Great News for
America

The Constitution, Freedom and Prosperity are Coming Back!

Gerard Francis Lameiro, Ph.D.

Author of *Renewing America and Its Heritage of Freedom*

D1367929

May One Nation under God

Indivisible with Liberty and Justice for All

Live in

Morality and Freedom

Peace and Prosperity

This book is dedicated to

America and to all Americans

Table of Contents

List of Figures

Preface

A Heartfelt Reason for Writing this Book. I'm writing this book from my heart to the hearts of all Americans. This book represents my understanding of American History, my analysis of the present, and my vision for America's optimistic future. That vision is for morality and freedom, peace and prosperity, for all Americans.

America, we have a great future.

America's truth began with its Founding Fathers and the Revolutionary War. It lives on in the Declaration of Independence that provides us with our moral principles, and in the Constitution that provides us with our political principles and guarantees all of our liberties.

America's truth began with the exceptional idea that God is the Author of our Liberty, that liberty was given by God to the people, and then was loaned by the people to its elected representatives for limited purposes, for a limited time, when the representatives served the people faithfully and morally. In stark contrast across time and geography, the leaders of non-exceptional nations reigned more or less supreme over their subjects, and grudgingly gave limited freedoms, for limited purposes, for limited times, to their subjects.

American Exceptionalism has never been the norm around the world.

America's truth continues on throughout all of the nation's moral and political challenges, all of the nation's wars and strife, and all the nation's economic crises and hardships that this nation has met with valor, endured with courage, and overcame with fortitude and hard work in its 240-year history.

America is at a critical crossroads today. Americans are morally outraged because they believe America has gone way off track. Americans sense a growing and grave moral, political and economic crisis. Americans are concerned that our nation might not survive, or might not survive as a free nation. Americans worry that we are losing our religious freedom, political freedom, and economic freedom.

Americans sense that this crisis stems from politicians and others who have abandoned America's founding documents; who have foregone morality and freedom; who have overseen cronyism, corruption, and the intoxication of power; and who are quite literally ruining and destroying the greatest nation ever to exist on this planet. They are justifiably and deeply concerned for America.

My answer to those who think America's greatest days are over, and my answer to those who think America's days as a free nation are over, is simple and direct. NO WAY.

The American people will not let this happen. The American people will take action in voting booths across the nation to realign political parties and political institutions as they see fit to reestablish morality and freedom. They have done so in the past. They will do it again. That's why my vision for America is filled with enthusiasm, optimism and energy.

Indeed, America will survive and America will remain free. America will continue to be the greatest, most creative, most innovative, most productive, and most generous nation in the history of the world. It will provide the greatest opportunities for its citizens, and it will provide the best future imaginable for its children and grandchildren. American Exceptionalism is alive and well, and it will continue to thrive as we move forward in the 21st century and beyond.

Freedom vs. the Ism's of Failure. It is worth noting why Americans have felt threatened as we approach the critical presidential election of 2016. We can place blame on what I call compactly the ism's of failure. The ism's of failure are: progressive socialism, socialism, Marxism, communism, and anarchism. In a nutshell, these ism's of failure preach their own gospel of secular atheism and agnosticism (two more ism's) that eschew morality and traditional family values, as well as religious freedom, political freedom, and economic freedom. They prefer to substitute the Rule of Man for the Rule of Law. They prefer centralized authoritative government to our Constitution and freedom for all individuals.

The purpose of this book is to refresh all of our collective memories about the fundamental goodness, integrity, and strength of America and its founding moral and political principles, as well as to see clearly through the fog of our current, grave national moral, political and economic crisis. Regrettably, most Americans believe our government is corrupt, our system is not responsive to the voters, and we are moving substantially off track. There are valid reasons for these enormous concerns, and more importantly, there are powerful core principles we can follow and common sense solutions we can achieve to the large issues we face. I detail both the principles and the solutions in this book.

In truth and confidence, I envision a refreshed and reinvigorated America whose founding documents are once again revered, respected, adhered to, and followed closely. This morally renewed nation based on freedom, peace and prosperity will be restored as a result of the upcoming critical presidential election of 2016. Along with that renewal of the American spirit will come the dawning of the next American Constitutional Era that I call the Conservative Era.

Progressive socialism, socialism, Marxism, communism, and anarchism are the political models of failure in today's struggling world. They are the modern day soft and hard tyrannies that oppress individuals and stagnate or eliminate economic growth. All lack a framework for true morality and freedom. All fail spiritually, culturally, politically and economically. All bring pain and suffering to mankind. All lead to moral and economic bankruptcy.

In the long run, only through force and/or deception can they hold on to power. The question for these political models of failure is how long before they deplete the wealth of a nation, and how long before they cause a nation to slide into bankruptcy. There is no other answer because they only consume wealth created in the private sector, and never produce wealth in the public sector.

While these political models of failure often make grandiose promises to those who succumb to these modern day forms of deception, corruption and tyranny, they always fail to deliver on these same lofty promises.

Many have been seduced by the ism's of failure. Many have succumbed to their unrealistic promises and their unending lies. Even those who are Christian often have been subtly seduced by socialism's offer to help the poor, neglecting the fact that their method robs their supposed beneficiaries of dignity and self-worth, while forcing them into a life of utter dependency on the whims of big government. Socialism will give the crumbs of aid to keep citizens permanently dependent, but never the food of substance to allow them to become free and independent and prosperous.

The morality and freedom our Founding Fathers built on the eastern shores of America in the late 1700's offers us the antithesis of the ism's of failure. American Exceptionalism is the path to success and victory.

Freedom – religious freedom, political freedom, economic freedom – will always lead to spiritual and material growth. The ism's of failure will always lead to moral and economic bankruptcy.

America's Future is Bright. My vision for America is optimistic and bright. This book describes the historical events and current events that are leading up to the critical presidential election of 2016. It will make ten surprising predictions that occur before, during, and after this critical presidential election. You will see that America's future is indeed bright and optimistic. Enjoy the book I have written from my heart to your heart. Enjoy America's bright future.

Introduction

There is great news for America. The Constitution, freedom and prosperity are all coming back.

Get ready for some big election year surprises. If my predictions are correct (and I think they are), the critical presidential election of 2016 will be nothing like you've seen before in your lifetime, even if you've lived through many different elections. In fact, it's shaping up to be the most profound presidential election since the critical election of 1896, an event that took place 120 years ago.

This book makes ten surprising predictions that are bold and powerful. These are stunning predictions, predictions about America, predictions about the 2016 presidential election, and predictions whose impact go far beyond this election. Indeed, this book predicts some historic events for America that will take place before, during and after the 2016 presidential election. Those events will positively impact America for decades to come.

Great News for America offers an innovative and unique approach to understanding the forthcoming critical presidential election of 2016. It looks at all seven American Constitutional Eras from 1789 through 2016, along with all associated critical presidential elections that bracket those American Constitutional Eras. It culls out the reasons that triggered each successive, new American Constitutional Era and each new critical presidential election. Importantly, it identifies a repeating pattern that can be used to predict new American Constitutional Eras and imminent critical presidential elections before they happen.

Rather than looking at the results of an election in the rear-view mirror as most political election books do, *Great News for America* takes the opposite approach. Based on knowledge of American political election dynamics from 1789 until now, it projects forward to the present day and attempts to make lively and informative judgements on the likelihood of how the current election will play out. This long-term analysis differs markedly from the short-term polling process most voters and citizens are accustomed to getting for predicting election results.

Great News for America provides insights into America, into its political history, and into its voters and their deeply-held beliefs on morality and freedom. It also clearly shows how voters in America are ultimately in charge; how they expect their political parties and political institutions to act; and how voters will decisively make parties and politicians accountable to themselves.

Millions of Americans will be surprised (possibly shocked) by the events surrounding the critical presidential election of 2016. I hope *Great News for America* will shed new light for you on the historic and critical presidential election of 2016 that I envision with my study of presidential elections and current events. It's time to get a front row seat for some profound and surprising American history about to be made.

Part I

Historical Events and Current Events that are setting the Stage for the Critical Presidential Election of 2016

Chapter 1

Historical Events and American Constitutional Eras

Looking ahead, the 2016 presidential election will be a run-away conservative election landslide. In fact, it will be the third conservative election landslide in less than a decade. We are now in the midst of a growing conservative movement whose results already include two recent conservative election landslides – the landslide that captured the House of Representatives in historic proportions in 2010, followed by the similarly historic takeover of the Senate in a conservative landslide in 2014. The stage is set for the third conservative election landslide, the capture of the White House in 2016, with a compelling conservative mandate and an overwhelming Presidential Electoral College victory, not seen since President Ronald Reagan won re-election in 1984 with 525 out of a possible 538 electoral votes.

Of course, the 1984 conservative landslide itself confirmed another conservative landslide, the critical election of 1980, in which Ronald Reagan was swept into office with an enormous Presidential Electoral College victory consisting of 489 out of 538 electoral votes, leaving only a handful of States and the District of Columbia for then President Jimmy Carter to carry.

This third conservative landslide, the 2016 presidential election landslide, will happen despite the fact that the early polls in 2015 indicated a boring, mundane and lackluster campaign with the presumed front-running nominees having names and policies from the past as well as polling numbers that were roughly equivalent. Certainly, those are the ingredients for a dreary and uninspiring election to be sure. While polls can often accurately shed light on short term and secular trends, longer term and paradigm-shifting, long wave changes can go completely undetected and simply slip under the normal analytic radar of forecasters and experts alike.

Truly, the 2016 presidential election will be the most crucial, significant and decisive election in 120 years, quite literally a once-in-a-century election. It will represent a monumental turning point in American History – a conservative blockbuster victory and a mega-mandate for freedom for the rest of the 21st century and beyond. It also punctuates the complete end of the modern socialist, Progressive Era (and error) that began in 1896 and continued influencing other American Constitutional Eras throughout the 20th century. Indeed, this presidential election, unlike nearly all other presidential elections in our history with the exceptions of 1789 and 1896, will mark a powerful and robust inflection point in American History and indeed, all of Western Civilization for likely another century and beyond.

What Causes a New American Constitutional Era?

For Americans, these words taken from the Declaration of Independence form the moral principles for America's political system:

> WE hold these Truths to be self-evident, that all Men are created equal, that they are endowed by their Creator with certain unalienable Rights, that among these are Life, Liberty, and the Pursuit of Happiness – That to secure these Rights, Governments are instituted among Men, deriving their just Powers from the Consent of the Governed …

They are not just idealistic words that are divorced from reality. They are truly core moral principles written into the DNA of America's moral framework, the Declaration of Independence. Plus, they are the core political principles written into the DNA of America's political framework, the Constitution.

America loves liberty. Truly, Americans are freedom-loving people. Americans are also moral people. They expect their government to be moral and to follow moral principles. They expect their fellow citizens to act morally as well. America's 240 years of political history prove these points.

Morality and freedom are inextricably linked together as I have discussed in some detail in my book: *Renewing America and Its Heritage of Freedom*. The moral case for freedom is clear and concise and comes from America's Judeo-Christian heritage.[1] It's no wonder that morality and freedom play such a significant role in American History. Parenthetically, it's also no wonder why the Christian Church is attacked so vigorously by those who seek to eliminate morality and freedom from the lives of citizens.

During periods when our government acts morally and protects our liberty, the electorate remains relatively content. Voters literally feel free to go about their daily lives, and strive in their own unique and individual ways to pursue happiness.

On the other hand, from time to time, American government can stray from its moral principles. It can go too far off track. It can cease to respect the freedom of individuals. It can abandon the morality voters expect. If and when it does fail to adhere to its moral principles, then a powerful, moral outrage develops among citizens. It's as if a silent, calm, peaceful majority of Americans wake up and shout: "Enough!"

This collective reaction, this intense moral passion, can rock the very foundations of our political parties and our political institutions. Indeed, when the structures, functions and powers of our political institutions get out of synchronization with American social forces and political constituencies, we can, and often, we will suddenly reach a tipping point for political change. If this happens, we can expect to witness dramatic realignments in both our political parties and our political institutions.

When Americans get upset and dissatisfied with government performance because moral principles are not being followed, big changes tend to happen. This is the primary reason why political parties and political institutions experience drastic realignments from time to time. This is also the cause of new American Constitutional Eras. In fact, political party realignments, political institution realignments and the creation of new American Constitutional Eras are often closely related as we will see in the next several sections.

In a parallel way, if political candidates for office from a given party consistently make promises to voters over a series of elections, serious expectations are set in the minds of these voters. If these consistent promises made to voters are also consistently broken over a period of several elections, the future doesn't bode well for that political party. Woe to the political party that continually promises and fails to deliver on its promises. It frustrates voters enormously and presages the party's ultimate demise or in the very least, significant restructuring.

Looking throughout American History, we see that changes happen remarkably often in American politics. In fact, there seems to be a new American Constitutional Era about every 32 to 36 years (or about every eight or nine presidential elections). Of course, there are a few exceptions. But, America generally renews its political system every 36 years, give or take a few years. You might say that it's America's way to avoid violent revolutions, although the Civil War was one time that the system failed to keep the peace.

In truth, America loves freedom and expects morality. When the government fails morally to promote, protect and defend freedom, the ensuing moral outrage will eventually generate realignments in political parties and political institutions. In some cases, the moral outrage will be so great that a new American Constitutional Era will emerge and will restore America's political equanimity.

American Constitutional Eras, Critical Elections and Major Party Realignments

Throughout history, as a nation, America has experienced a few Constitutional Eras and several critical elections, party realignments and political realignments. The 2016 presidential election is shaping up to be the dawning of a new American Constitutional Era, the Conservative Era, as I call it, as well as a critical election in American History. In addition, it will likely result in profound party realignments during this election process.

Samuel P. Huntington speaks of four distinct eras in American History that "involve the profound upheaval in the overall relations between social forces and political institutions."[2] These are the

Revolutionary Era, the Jacksonian Era, the Progressive Era, and the "era of sixes and sevens" or the "S&S Years." The latter S&S Years is a stand-in name for the 1960s and early 1970s,[3] a time that has been difficult for historians to fully comprehend and to label accurately.

Ken Kollman discusses another way to slice and dice political time periods throughout American history. He describes six party systems as well as various major events that impacted our two party system, such as the War of 1812, the Civil War, and the New Deal.[4]

While Huntington and Kollman provide useful analyses of American political history, this book presents a more comprehensive look at American Constitutional Eras and tees up the new Conservative Era that I envision. Indeed, we are all witnessing the dawning of the new Conservative Era in the current 2016 presidential election campaign. This information is presented as a basis and foundation for my prediction of the new Conservative Era and as a way of setting the stage for this guide to the 2016 presidential election itself. It is not intended to review American political history in-depth. That would be a separate book, all its own.

Here's a quick look at how I categorize American Constitutional Eras and the critical elections associated with them. Figure 1 summarizes these eras in a simple chart. Note that all elections listed in the chart are critical elections in American History. The following few sections will summarize the seven American Constitutional Eras.

Constitutional Era, Jacksonian Era, Civil War Era

Constitutional Era (1800 – 1828). The first American Constitutional Era starts with the critical election of 1800. This was the first presidential election in which the opposition party was elected. Thomas Jefferson, a Democrat-Republican, was elected president and Aaron Burr (also a Democrat-Republican) was elected vice president. The three Federalist candidates under consideration, John Adams, Charles Cotesworth Pinckney and John

Figure 1 – American Constitutional Eras and Critical Elections

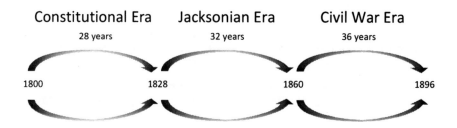

Constitutional Era   Jacksonian Era   Civil War Era

28 years   32 years   36 years

1800   1828   1860   1896

Progressive Era   Constitutional Activism Era   Entitlement Era

36 years   32 years   16 years

1896   1932   1964   1980

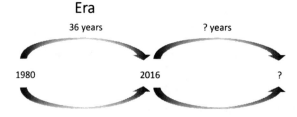

Anti-Constitutional Era   Conservative Era

36 years   ? years

1980   2016   ?

Jay, all didn't receive sufficient electoral votes.[5]

One of the primary issues during this critical election was the tug-of-war between Federalists who sought to maintain a strong central government versus the Democrat-Republicans (or Jeffersonian-Republicans) that believed in States' rights. High taxes were also a top campaign issue.[6]

The Constitutional Era was a time period in which the newly created nation and its fledgling Federal government got established. During this era, it took root. It needed a somewhat strong centralized government initially. Otherwise, it might fail quickly and the States would lack unity and coherence. America needed the United States because it required "united" States to cooperate, to survive and to thrive.

Yet, the States also required a solid degree of autonomy to maintain their own identity and uniqueness. Some citizens were concerned that the Federal government might become a virtual monarchy. Their experience with Great Britain left a bitter taste for another monarchy.

The Constitutional Era saw the alignment of power behind the Federal government change dramatically, from mercantile and business interests to those who supported an agrarian society in the South and West. The critical election of 1800 saw a political realignment of social forces and the relative power of competing parties realign as well. These changes would largely remain in force for 28 years.[7]

This power shift might very well be one of the reasons why America succeeded as a nation. It was an opportunity to bring others into the Federal power-sharing equation, strengthening the United States while still encouraging States' rights.

Of importance during this early American Constitutional Era was the role of the Supreme Court. John Adams, who was the sitting president during the critical election of 1800 and who lost another term as president to Thomas Jefferson, appointed John Marshall as the Chief Justice of the United States, prior to the swearing-in of

Thomas Jefferson. The purpose was to make the Supreme Court a Federalist stronghold for a strong centralized Federal government, even though the executive branch fell into the hands of the Democrat-Republicans.[8]

In the precedent-setting and legally famous decision of *Marbury v. Madison (1803)*, the Chief Justice clearly articulated the opinion that because the United States has a written Constitution, the Supreme Court had the power to declare laws unconstitutional. Here are his words: "The powers of the legislature are defined and limited; and that those limits may not be mistaken, or forgotten, the constitution is written."[9]

This was clearly the Constitutional Era in American History.

Jacksonian Era (1828 – 1860). The second American Constitutional Era starts with the critical election of Andrew Jackson in 1828 and ends with the critical election of 1860.[10] The election of 1828 was a critical election in American History, but for far different reasons than the critical election of 1800.

The seeds of the Jacksonian Era took root in the early 1820's. Andrew Jackson recognized a time of corruption in government.[11] He feared that increasing centralized power would ultimately rob the people of their liberties. His themes during this time period centered on "virtue, religion and morality."[12]

Of course, Americans rallied around those themes in 1828 when they ultimately sought presidential leadership. Indeed, America's moral outrage aligned closely with Andrew Jackson's assessment of the situation.

What characterized the critical presidential election of 1828?

For one thing, it was a popular election with considerable enthusiasm for General Andrew Jackson, clearly still a war hero. Indeed, it seemed much like a voter revolution.[13] While voter turnout in the 1824 election was a mere 26.9% of eligible voters,[14] the critical election of 1828 saw a voter turnout that exceeded that number by more than double. Voter turnout was a hefty 57.6%.

More than 800,000 additional voters participated in the 1828 critical election over the 1824 election. That's quite an increase when you realize that the total population in America was just over 12 million people in 1828.[15]

In addition to being a popular election with considerable interest and involvement of voters, it was also a critical election because there was a fundamental party realignment. The Democrat-Republicans under Andrew Jackson with the help of Martin Van Buren and John Calhoun morphed into the Jackson Party or the "Democratic" Republican Party (note the slight difference in name from the Democrat-Republican Party to the Democratic Republican Party) or simply, the Democratic Party. In 1832, the Democratic Party name stuck and it became the commonly used name for that party from then on.[16]

Of interest, John Quincy Adams' Democrat-Republicans became the "National" Republican Party. The critical election of 1828 also saw the formation of America's first third party, the Anti-Masonic Party that sought freedom of opportunity for individuals.[17] By 1834, the National Republican Party had become known as the Whig Party, or simply the Whigs, when the National Republicans joined forces with the Anti-Masonic Party and others then led at the time by John Calhoun.[18]

Jacksonian Democrats favored policies similar to Thomas Jefferson, namely, States' rights and the needs of ordinary citizens. In contrast, the National Republicans sought a strong central government much like the Federalists did prior to 1800. They also advocated for the material strength of the nation.[19]

Of significance, citizens became more involved in their government as political parties fostered an avenue for their participation. The Jacksonian Era was characterized by widespread democratic involvement with committees and organization from the national level to the state level, to the county and local levels. Also, parties became the vehicles for staffing government jobs, encouraging strong citizen loyalty to a particular party.[20]

In fact, the critical presidential election of 1828 was touted as the:

"triumph of the great principle of self-government."[21] Many saw the election as protecting America from the three great dangers of "aristocracy, privilege, and corruption."[22]

The needs of ordinary citizens, States' rights, and the chance to become more involved in government at all levels seemed to resonate with voters. Clearly, morality and freedom were best served in the minds of Americans by electing the Jacksonian Democrats during this era. Their moral enthusiasm was palpable and political energies were engaged in both political party realignment and political institution realignment.

As a result, during this era Jacksonian Democrats dominated presidential and Congressional elections. Out of eight presidential elections from 1828 to 1856, the Democrats won six out of eight presidential elections and lost only two elections to the Whigs[23] – William Henry Harrison in 1840[24] and Zachary Taylor in 1848.[25]

The Jacksonian Era was a democratic period where citizen involvement grew tremendously and the role of our two-party system solidified and became a prominent feature of our American political system.[26]

Civil War Era (1860 – 1896). The Civil War Era is the third American Constitutional Era. It begins with the critical election of Abraham Lincoln in 1860 and ends with the critical election of William McKinley in 1896.

The critical election of 1860 was significant for a number of reasons including the fact that voter turnout was 81.2% of eligible voters, one of the highest voter turnouts in American History.[27] That in itself tells us how important voters viewed this election.

Of course, another reason for this election's significance is that this election was primarily about slavery. America was in turmoil at the time. Many Americans strongly opposed slavery and also opposed extending its usage even further to include new States entering the Union. Many other Americans favored allowing individual States to decide as they saw fit, essentially taking a States' rights approach to the debate. Some Americans hoped to find a compromise solution to the slavery question, perhaps thinking it would gradually be replaced over time with freedom for everyone. But, the moral outrage was great and many sought a faster answer to the slavery issue.[28]

The famous Missouri Compromise was one attempt to partially resolve the issue. With the Missouri Compromise, Congress decided to admit new States to the Union two at a time. It permitted one slave State (Missouri) and one free State (Maine) into the Union, while also following some other rules. In the infamous case *Dred Scott v. Sandford (1856)*, Chief Justice Roger Taney, a Southern partisan, effectively ruled the Federal government could not outlaw slavery in any State in America. This essentially made the Missouri Compromise unconstitutional.[29]

Interestingly, before the Dred Scott decision was handed down, Congress had actually already repealed the Missouri Compromise. Making it unconstitutional was a moot point, except for Dred Scott, the plaintiff in the case, who still sought his freedom. His case involved events that happened while the Missouri Compromise was still in place.[30]

The Dred Scott decision had wide-ranging effects on America. It created a great divide and controversy. It made the political party divisions deeper and more hurtful. Some even believe it took the Civil War to overturn this decision.[31]

Retrospectively, in a Constitutional sense, the Dred Scott decision was probably the very first time "substantive due process" was used by the Supreme Court to read into the Constitution something that originally did not appear in the Constitution. That's significant, as substantive due process has adversely impacted Supreme Court decisions since that time.[32]

With regard to the law, due process means that an individual is treated fairly from a Constitutional and statutory perspective. In other words, standard procedures and processes are applied and followed in a consistent manner for all citizens. In essence, that's part of the Rule of Law.

Substantive due process throws a wrinkle into the equation. With substantive due process, the substance or content of the Constitution or relevant statute is called into question. Indeed, activist Supreme Court justices (or judges in lower courts) can pick and choose what content is to be added or deleted from the Constitution or statute. Unfortunately, the concept of substantive due process substitutes the morality of justices for the morality of the people as evidenced by the Constitution or the Federal, State and local laws in question.[33]

Without question, slavery was the primary political issue of the day. So much so, that a Chief Justice needed to stretch the Constitution with an early version of substantive due process to fit his personal preference to see slavery continued.

Leading up to the critical election of 1860, political party power was ebbing and in considerable decline. As a result in part, many new third parties arose and were active for at least a short time. For example, the Know-Nothing Party was an anti-Catholic and anti-immigrant party. They believed Europeans were sending immigrants to America to harm our nation, holding down pay increases for American laborers because foreign workers would willingly work for less. For a time because they were politically neutral on slavery, the Know Nothings attracted those who did not take a stand on slavery from both the Democrat and Whig Parties.[34]

Other examples of third parties at the time were the Liberty Party that opposed slavery and the Constitutional Union Party that tried to side step the slavery question altogether by uniting voters around the Constitution. Ultimately, the Know Nothing Party, the Liberty Party, and the Constitutional Union Party all succumbed to the real tumult and deep dissension surrounding the issue of slavery.[35]

Of additional importance in the Civil Rights Era were the new amendments to the Constitution – the Thirteenth Amendment that abolished slavery; the Fourteenth Amendment that applied due process to the States; and the Fifteenth Amendment that prevented denial of voting rights based on race, color, or previous condition of servitude.

The Fourteenth Amendment would subsequently have a grave impact on future Supreme Court decisions after it became a means of applying the preferences of justices over the Constitution and statutes with substantive due process in a wide array of decisions. It also gave the Supreme Court considerable power over the States when it was interpreted to include applying the Bill of Rights to the States.[36]

The Civil War Era, the related critical election of 1860, and the various associated political party realignments were all fueled by the moral outrage and indignation over slavery. This new era was caused by many citizens across the two major party lines that were both morally and vocally upset over the obvious dissonance between our founding moral principles, enshrined in the Declaration of Independence, and the continuation of slavery.

Unfortunately, the terrible institution of slavery held over from past millennia had not been extinguished completely during the formation of our nation in 1776, or during the drafting of the Constitution in 1789. But, by 1860, many Americans demanded that slavery cease to exist. America's love for liberty and expectation of morality could no longer tolerate the centuries' old practice of slavery.

Progressive Era, Constitutional Activism Era

Progressive Era (1896 – 1932). The fourth American Constitutional Era is the Progressive Era that spans the time period from the critical election of 1896 to the critical election of 1932. It lasted about 36 years.

In the critical election of 1896, William McKinley (Republican) was elected over William Jennings Bryan (Democrat) and several third party candidates, including John Palmer (National Democrat or Gold Democrat), Joshua Levering (Prohibition) and Charles Matchett (Socialist Labor). The voter turnout of 79.3% was high that year – an indication of the importance of the election.[37]

The year 1896 was a tough year for America. To many citizens, it felt like a year of national crisis. In fact, the immediate years preceding the critical election of 1896 were characterized by political and economic distress and uncertainty among voters. For example, Americans experienced the panic of 1893 that saw about 15,000 businesses go bankrupt. Americans also faced high unemployment, along with political and social unrest.[38]

With the Pullman strike, violent labor clashes and the marches on Washington, law and order became an issue on the minds of voters. There were also considerable debates over gold and silver standards, with Republicans strongly favoring gold and Democrats and Populists wanting a silver standard.[39]

The political and economic problems America faced before the critical election of 1896 led some voters to even wonder if America and its political institutions would survive.[40] That's how serious the problems were in those days.

Albert B. Hart noted that there was impatience with the ability of our system to bring about the change of laws needed to fix the political and economic problems using "legal and constitutional methods" suggesting our Constitutional republic was somehow inadequate or badly broken.[41]

Moral outrage among citizens increased significantly because of the perception that our government was not getting the job done. Citizens often felt that the great economic downturn they were experiencing was not being adequately addressed under the Democratic administration of President Grover Cleveland.

Partly as a result of the political and economic problems, progressive ideas entered the national debate at this time, articulated largely by Democrats, Populists and Socialists. Of interest, the progressive ideas seemed to gain a foothold (but, not a stronghold) among supporters across the spectrum of political parties. But rather than cause a Democrat victory, voters in 1896 were turned off by the Democrats for a variety of reasons. Separately, urban, professional and managerial workers gravitated toward the Republican Party with their message of prosperity through a gold standard, economic stability and traditional cultural values. While progressive ideas appeared to offer some hope to some voters, the progressive messengers were generally rejected in the critical election of 1896.[42]

The Progressive Era also saw the rise of the Progressive Party (or Bull Moose Party) in 1912. It was created by former President Theodore Roosevelt after he left the Republican Party. For a third-party, he actually did well coming in with over 29% of the vote.[43]

Being a strong proponent of progressive ideas, Theodore Roosevelt fought for his concept of a better democracy, encapsulated in the term "New Nationalism."[44] In some ways, Woodrow Wilson espoused similar progressive ideas in his campaign speeches and political philosophy called "The New Freedom."[45]

But, both of these "New" approaches had a serious flaw. They both required flaunting the Constitutional tradition and other long-standing systems and processes that America had relied on during its first century. Further, to promote progressive policies, questionable Supreme Court decisions ultimately would be required in the 1930's.

Nevertheless, three substantive progressive areas of so-called reform were addressed by progressives during the Progressive Era. First, progressives were concerned with large concentrations of economic power, the trusts.[46] Theodore Roosevelt, for example, sought to balance the power of big corporations with big government. One strategy on the part of progressives to deal with the concentration of wealth was to initiate an income tax, especially on corporations.[47]

Second, progressives also believed in more direct democracy. They specifically sought to reduce the power and influence of political parties reasoning that special interests were effectively pulling the strings of political parties and essentially reducing the power of individual citizens.[48]

Progressive interest in "direct democracy" reforms took a host of other practices as well, many living on into the 21st century. These included the direct election of Senators (as opposed to selection by State legislatures as originally called for in Article 1 Section 3 of the Constitution), direct initiatives, recalls and referendum elections.[49]

Still other ideas included: direct primaries and non-partisan elections. Direct primaries, in turn, were the forerunner of "candidate-centered" political campaigns that developed later in the 20th century.[50]

The third and final progressive area of so-called reform was in the arena of social welfare. Specifically, progressives argued for insurance to protect workers from unemployment, accidents, sickness and old age.[51] In today's parlance, some of these would be labeled unemployment insurance, ObamaCare and Social Security.

Of special significance in the critical presidential election of 1896 was an innovative change in political strategy and tactics. From roughly the 1850's onward, political campaigns were generally characterized by a military style of campaigning that featured the emotional appeal of mass meetings, torchlight parades, bonfires, banners, and brass bands. Instead in 1896, Republicans followed an entirely new approach to political campaigning called the "campaign of education." It was more of an educational appeal to find new voters, rather than an emotional appeal to motivate existing supporters and thereby, get out the usual expected voters.[52]

The "campaign of education" included publicity and advertising and was geared to educating voters on new solutions to the many issues challenging the nation at the time. It amounted to the merchandising of ideas.[53] Apparently, the new strategy worked as evidenced by the high voter turnout mentioned earlier. Many "educated" voters took part in the election of 1896.

One final point that deals with the candidate himself is worth recognizing. Called the "prophet of prosperity,"[54] William McKinley had an uncanny ability to pull together a cohesive message on jobs and the idea of "the full dinner pail."[55] His emphasis and focus on jobs, a vital issue in the hard economic times of the 1890's, resonated with voters. He was able to articulate a positive economic theme that remarkably unified many of the other issues in the campaign, including sound money, the gold standard, tariffs, and even immigration, around the central issue of jobs.[56] To his credit, he garnered strong support from the electorate.

Political constituencies and support for political parties was clearly and dramatically realigned in the election of 1896 fueled by moral outrage over the state of the union and substantial economic challenges. This realignment would result in Republican presidential election victories throughout the Progressive Era, except for the elections of Woodrow Wilson in 1912 and 1916. The time period from 1896 through 1932, with its emphasis on progressive ideas, its implementation of progressive approaches to government, and its impact then and later on our Constitution, was the Progressive Era in American History.

Constitutional Activism Era (1932 – 1964). The Constitutional Activism Era began with the critical election of 1932 and ended with the critical election of 1964. It followed closely on the heels of the Progressive Era and it was characterized by an assault on the Constitution by activist Supreme Court justices that chose to implement a progressive philosophy on key decisions. It also coincided with, and was supported by, Franklin D. Roosevelt's progressive New Deal that took place during the Constitutional Activism Era.

During the presidential election of 1932, America was once again in crisis. This time it was as a result of the 1929 stock market crash and the ensuing Great Depression that was exacerbated in part by the deflationary monetary policy of the Federal Reserve.[57] The Federal Reserve itself was another product of the Progressive Era. It was signed into law by Woodrow Wilson in 1913.[58]

Instead of providing more liquidity to the American Economy, the Feds chose to preside over the decline in the monetary supply. This lack of money in the economy helped to trigger a wave of bank failures that numbered in the hundreds. During the three year period leading up to 1932, about one third of the nation's money supply was lost.[59]

The Great Contraction of the monetary supply along with several other government missteps starved the American Economy during the tragic depression years causing undue suffering and despair. The Great Depression was a testament to the inability of the Federal government to effectively micro-manage our economy during those challenging years.[60]

In the fall of 1932, unemployment reached a staggering 23.6%. In some large cities, about one third of people didn't have jobs. Many of those who were employed worked for extremely low wages and/or for fewer than normal hours per week. Poverty was rampant. Conditions were appalling. Citizens were desperate.[61]

In the critical election of 1932, Franklin D. Roosevelt rose to an easy landslide victory on his well-known campaign theme: "Happy days are here again." The Democrat Party, which had been the minority party during the Progressive Era, was transformed into the majority party as a result of the critical election of 1932.[62]

Progressive policies and inappropriate government intervention in the economy helped cause and extend the longevity of the Great Depression. Both Republican and Democrat parties were partially to blame during the Progressive Era. The real culprit was progressive government. Ironically, the moral outrage of citizens and the sorry state of the economy led them to elect Franklin D. Roosevelt and with that election to get more progressive intervention in the economy. Rather than blaming Herbert Hoover and the Republican Party for the Great Depression, progressive policies and big government were truly at fault.

Prior to the Constitutional Activism Era, the Supreme Court generally followed the principle of Federalism built into the Constitution.[63] It can be explained rather easily by reading the Constitution's Tenth Amendment:

> The powers not delegated to the United States by the Constitution, nor prohibited by it to the States, are reserved to the States respectively, or to the people.

Federalism is vitally important to the American people and to their individual liberty because it limits the power and jurisdiction of the Federal government to those powers specifically delegated by the Constitution to the United States (that is, to the Federal government, as opposed to the States individually).

Why is Federalism critical to assuring individual liberty? Let's consider an example. Suppose your State decides to make smoking cigarettes completely illegal within the confines of your State. If you have a great desire to smoke cigarettes, what can you do? For one, you can always leave your State and move to another State that doesn't ban smoking. You retain the freedom to live where you choose to live in the pursuit of your happiness.

But, consider the situation if Federalism were not built into the Constitution. In this case, if the Federal government decides to make smoking cigarettes illegal, your only recourse is to move to another country, a much higher hurdle and barrier to overcome for most people.

Federalism is one more mechanism within the Constitution to protect our liberties. But, it caused a Constitutional crisis during the Constitutional Activism Era.[64]

Because of Federalism, Franklin D. Roosevelt faced a Supreme Court that struck down various New Deal economic regulations. Why? They exceeded the powers given to the Federal government by the Constitution.[65] This led to President Roosevelt's infamous attempt to pack the Supreme Court, an attempt that ultimately failed.[66]

One associate justice, Owen Roberts, in an historic change of outlook became the Supreme Court justice that changed the Supreme Court from conservative to progressive. "The switch in time that saved nine" made Roosevelt's plan to pack the court no longer necessary.

In the *National Labor Relations Board v. Jones & Laughlin Steel Corp. (1937)* decision, the Supreme Court upheld the National Labor Relations Act that regulated labor and management in businesses involved in local commerce.[67]

While Article I, Section 8 of the Constitution clearly gave power to the Federal government to regulate commerce among the States, the Jones & Laughlin decision now extended that power to include local commerce because it presumably might have some effects on interstate commerce. The bottom line was that judicial activism now gave the Federal government virtual control over the economic life of all Americans.[68]

With Franklin D. Roosevelt's election eventually came the appointment of additional activist Supreme Court justices. These included Hugo Black, Stanley Reed, Felix Frankfurter and William O. Douglas. He also elevated associate justice Harlan Stone to chief justice.[69]

Later, in 1953, President Dwight D. Eisenhower appointed Earl Warren to be Chief Justice of the Supreme Court. His appointments allowed judicial activism to largely continue throughout the rest of the Constitutional Activism Era. In particular, Justices Black and Douglas appeared to think social results trumped Constitutional principles.[70]

With some notable exceptions, the Warren Court decisions tended to be written along egalitarian and redistributionist lines. Generally, these decisions showcased a progressive philosophy that was implemented with judicial activism. In many ways, the Warren Court might better be termed a social engineering body or a legislator of social policy, rather than a traditional and impartial court of justice.[71]

Overall, the fifth American Constitutional Era, the Constitutional Activism Era, saw the Supreme Court stop its previous protection of Federalism, abandon economic due process, and attempt to decide cases using a progressive, egalitarian and redistributionist philosophy. The Constitution and liberty both suffered.

In the Constitutional Activism Era, economic crisis led to moral outrage on the part of the citizens and a critical election. Both party realignment and political realignment took place. In this case, the New Deal policies of Franklin D. Roosevelt also eventually triggered a Constitutional crisis that resulted in an extended period of judicial activism. This was the Constitutional Activism Era. It would end in 1964.

Entitlement Era, Anti-Constitutional Era

Entitlement Era (1964 – 1980). The sixth American Constitutional Era is the Entitlement Era. It is the shortest of the American Constitutional Eras, lasting only 16 years. It began with the critical election of 1964 and the landslide election of Lyndon B. Johnson over Barry Goldwater. It ended with the critical election of 1980 and another landslide election, the election of Ronald Reagan over Jimmy Carter.

Of note, during the Entitlement Era, Ronald Reagan came on the scene with his 1964 speech entitled: "A Time for Choosing" that supported Barry Goldwater's presidential campaign. This speech thrust him into a conservative leadership position that would eventually gain him the 1980 Republican presidential nomination and presidential election. In fact, it almost gave him the nomination over Gerald Ford in the difficult and closely fought 1976 Republican presidential race. So, Ronald Reagan rose to prominence during the Entitlement Era and his conservative presence bracketed this era.

His words rang true in 1964, were true in 1980, and still ring true for the 2016 presidential election campaign:

> This is the issue of this election: whether we believe in our capacity for self-government or whether we abandon the American Revolution and confess that a little intellectual elite in a far-distant capital can plan our lives for us better that we can plan them ourselves.

> The Founding Fathers knew a government can't control the economy without controlling people. And they knew when a government sets out to do that, it must use force and coercion to achieve its purpose. So we have come to a time for choosing.

> You and I have a rendezvous with destiny. We will preserve for our children this, the last best hope of man on earth, or we will sentence them to take the first step into a thousand years of darkness.[72]

The critical election of 1964 pivoted on that crucial issue, a time for choosing, and on the articulation of the conservative Constitutional message of morality and freedom vs. immorality and eventual socialist tyranny. But, other issues would prevail for a time. Goldwater was to lose in a landslide. Yet, his campaign was to signal and foreshadow the critical election of 1980 and Reagan's 1980 landslide, as well as his encore landslide to follow in 1984.

In 1964, America was dealing with political stresses from many different directions. Americans were still reeling and recovering from the loss of President John F. Kennedy who had been assassinated in November 1963 in Dallas. Americans were also trying to comprehend and deal with the Civil Rights Act of 1964 that impacted party loyalty in the South and to varying degrees, in other regions as well. Social troubles including riots (such as the Harlem Riot in July 1964), big city ghettos, and crime were all on the minds of voters. While simmering in the background, Vietnam had yet to become a major issue during the critical election of 1964.[73]

In addition to these events, there was an ideological battle brewing between Lyndon B. Johnson who sought to wage a "War on Poverty" by creating a "Great Society" that would take on poverty with government welfare programs and the Republicans. Republicans were against both big government in general and "creeping socialism" in particular.[74]

The 1964 election also highlighted the fault line dividing the Republican Party between the so called eastern liberal establishment and conservatives from the West. Eastern liberal establishment leaders at the time included Nelson Rockefeller (NY), William W. Scranton (PA) and George Romney (MI), while Barry Goldwater (AZ) and Ronald Reagan (CA) represented the conservatives.[75] This split would continue on until the present day.

During the Entitlement Era, the Twenty-Fourth Amendment was ratified in 1964. It barred poll taxes for any Federal elections or primaries. The Twenty-Sixth Amendment that allowed eighteen year olds to vote was also ratified during the Entitlement Era in 1971.

Of great significance to America from a Constitutional perspective, was a new entitlement or right given to Americans by the Supreme Court during the Entitlement Era. This so-called "Right of Privacy" was literally incorporated into Constitutional law out of the active minds of the Supreme Court justices. It had zero Constitutional legitimacy from a direct reading of the Constitution.[76]

The Right of Privacy was deemed to exist in the majority decision in a case known as *Griswold v. Connecticut (1965)*. The Supreme Court invalidated a little known and outdated law that prohibited the use of contraceptives. However, it didn't need to reach the Supreme Court for review. This law should have been removed from the books years earlier, as it is difficult to image any local police authorities that would intend to enforce it. Old, anachronistic laws sometimes live on for lack of interest and time to repeal them.[77]

Instead, the Supreme Court took up the matter and ruled on it. In the process, it created a new Right of Privacy. It was another case involving substantive due process where the justices read the Right of Privacy into the Constitution, where no previous Right of Privacy existed. *Griswold v. Connecticut (1965)* was a blatant illustration of judicial activism where the morality of justices took precedence over the morality of the people as evidenced by the Constitution or the Federal, State and local laws in question.[78]

The profound significance of the Right of Privacy was its later use in Constitutional law. In fact, the Right of Privacy with its open-ended, imprecise and nebulous meaning can be interpreted by justices in almost any way they choose. For example, the so-called Right of Privacy was used in the *Roe v. Wade (1973)* decision to justify a right to abortion, also nowhere to be found in the Constitution, and overturning numerous State laws dealing with abortion.[79]

In general, the Right of Privacy seems to be one more tool in the hands of progressives to coerce "lifestyle" socialism over traditional American, conservative family values. Indeed, the culture wars in America over recent decades might actually be the struggle of "lifestyle" socialism over America's traditional morality and freedom embedded in our Founding documents.[80]

The Entitlement Era truly saw America morph from a rules-based society to a rights-based society with a host of entitlements and rights. Former Speaker of the House and historian Newt Gingrich captured this time period accurately with this description:

> Since 1965, however, there has been a calculated effort by cultural elites to discredit this civilization and replace it with a culture of irresponsibility that is incompatible with American freedoms as we have known them.[81]

In truth, Lyndon B. Johnson and the Great Society launched the Entitlement Era. The Federal government gained the appearance of a new welfare state on the world stage. Entitlements were here to stay. The year 1965 featured: Medicare and Medicaid programs; Federal education assistance in the form of student loans and grants; Federal housing program development, along with rent subsidies; the Immigration and Nationality Act of 1965; and the National Endowment for the Arts as well as the National Endowment for the Humanities.[82]

Other cultural phenomena related to the Entitlement Era included the Sexual Revolution and the Pill. For the first time in 1965, our culture witnessed partial nudity in a mainstream movie. It was also the era that included the Free Speech Movement and the formation of the National Organization for Women (NOW).[83]

The critical election of 1964 saw two distinct and deeply divided portions of the electorate sensing intense moral outrage. Progressive socialists were upset over racial and Civil Rights concerns, while conservatives were profoundly troubled and disturbed by creeping socialism.

Progressives and conservatives developed and held diametrically opposed views on both morality and freedom. With the growing movement toward socialism, America experienced the Entitlement Era of 1964 through 1980.

Anti-Constitutional Era (1980 – 2016). The seventh American Constitutional Era, the Anti-Constitutional Era, begins with the critical election of 1980 and ends with the critical election of 2016.

As we have noted earlier, the critical election of 1980 was a landslide election. Ronald Reagan received 489 electoral votes, Jimmy Carter obtained 49 electoral votes, and third party candidate John Anderson didn't get a single electoral vote. Ronald Reagan carried 44 States, while Jimmy Carter won six States plus the District of Columbia, despite the fact that Jimmy Carter was the incumbent president in 1980.[84]

The Anti-Constitutional Era will end in another landslide election. This upcoming critical election of 2016, the subject of this book, will be described in subsequent chapters in some detail.

The critical election year of 1980 was once again a year of great crisis in America. It was preceded in March 1979 by the Three Mile Island nuclear power plant accident that fueled fears of catastrophe and sparked environmental hyperbole.[85] In July 1979, President Jimmy Carter gave his infamous "malaise" speech in which he stated Americans were suffering from a "crisis of confidence." In that speech, he implied Americans were at fault and had failed. Of course, instead many Americans believed it was just the opposite. It was the president who was the cause of the crisis of confidence and he had failed the American people.[86]

During 1980, four separate but related crises shook the American psyche. The first dealt with the American Economy. Economic woes were significant and palpable. Stagflation, the situation in which the economy suffered from economic stagnation and high inflation simultaneously, was obvious to voters.[87]

The Misery Index was one metric for calculating the pain Americans felt. The Misery Index was the unemployment rate added to the inflation rate. In 1980, the unemployment rate was 7.2%, inflation was 13.6%, and the Misery Index was 7.2% + 13.6% for a total of 20.8%.[88]

The top Federal income tax rate at the end of the Entitlement Era was 70%. When added with a 10% State tax rate, some Americans paid a marginal 80% of their incomes to Federal and State governments, dramatically lowering the incentive to work hard and to give the resulting earnings to big government.[89] Don't forget too that besides Federal and State income taxes, Americans also paid (and still pay) many other taxes. Sales taxes, property taxes, phone taxes, gasoline taxes, and taxes on utilities are just some examples of other taxes.

The second of the four crises facing Americans during the critical election of 1980 was in the realm of foreign policy. This was the time of the Iranian hostage crisis and the occupation of Afghanistan by Soviet troops.[90] It was seen as a time of American leadership failure in the world.

Then, there was the social crisis of the time. Voters saw government failing to adequately deal with crime and drugs. Plus, there was a concomitant decline in the family and family values. Numerous social indexes drastically declined during the Entitlement Era. The breakdown in the family and the breakdown in effective law enforcement all contributed to the social crisis felt by voters during the critical election of 1980.[91]

Finally, the fourth crisis was the overall crisis of confidence Americans felt.[92] It was as if the president and the Federal government had massively failed the American people. Of course, the government had done precisely that. It failed the American people.

Parenthetically, it is worth noting that there was also a lot of apocalyptic talk in the time leading up to the critical election of 1980. Environmentalists at that time were lamenting the devastating impacts of "global freezing" on the world.[93] Does that sound like the present day environmentalists? Indeed, it is precisely the same type of dire predictions we hear today, except the term "global warming" or the term "climate change" is substituted for "global freezing." It's a wonder anyone believes environmental claims of gloom and doom. They are consistently wrong.

The bottom line going into the critical election of 1980 was the high degree of moral outrage and the deep concern of the American people for the future of America … its moral, cultural and social future; its economic future, and its future as a global leader.

Ronald Reagan brought to the election his solid, across-the-board, conservative values and principles. Ronald Reagan believed in God. He also believed in the American people. He brought another intangible quality that would endear himself to the American people.

He manifestly expressed his whole-hearted enthusiasm and strong optimism for America. His vision for America was optimistic. America rewarded him with two landslide victories as a result.

Despite the critical election of 1980, Ronald Reagan's landslide victory, and the impact of political party dynamics, the critical election of 1980 ushered in the Anti-Constitutional Era. This might seem like a contradiction at first, but it isn't.

Recall how the critical election of 1896 worked. In that election, the progressive candidate, William Jennings Bryan, lost. Yet, as it turned out, 1896 was still the beginning of the Progressive Era.

Political party realignments and political institution realignments can take years to fully play out. They don't happen overnight.

Before jumping to the critical election of 2016, there is one more missing piece of the puzzle to provide. It is vital in understanding the predictions associated with the critical election of 2016. Indeed, one question must be answered: Why is the time period from 1980 to 2016 called the Anti-Constitutional Era?

The answer lies in the give and take of many individual election races, many divisive issues, many flawed court decisions, and many specific actions taken (or not taken) by the president and Congress, all that took place since the critical election of 1980. Let's do a quick overview of these factors.

The Anti-Constitutional Era is characterized by direct assaults on the spirit and letter of the Constitution. That's where its name comes from. Progressives during this era, while not completely rejecting the Constitution, largely ignored it, often circumvented it, or blatantly rejected its original intent with the lame excuse that it's a "living document."

We know that the Constitution's purpose is to protect our liberty. Liberty and freedom, and our fundamental Constitutional rights do not change. The Constitution is not a living, fluid, adjustable, changeable, variable, malleable, pliable, or flexible document. It's not any of those things. In truth, if a freedom is altered, its nature is changed. In reality, if a freedom is limited regardless of the intention or the excuse, its nature is changed. In particular, it loses its essence. It loses its universality and scope of application. It diminishes the power of all individuals to which it applies.

If we tamper with the Constitution, we impact our freedom. Progressives have systematically and directly assaulted our Constitution during the Anti-Constitutional Era in the Supreme Court, in the White House, and in Congress. Progressives have also promoted their Anti-Constitutional attacks in the mainstream media, in the entertainment media, and in our schools and universities. Progressives have been relentless in their pursuit of socialism throughout America.

While Anti-Constitutional attacks by progressives have been widespread and extensive, in the next few paragraphs, we give only a few examples. A more complete description of these attacks would fill its own book.

First, let's look at the Supreme Court. During the Anti-Constitutional Era, we have been beset with aggressive judicial activism. The role of a Supreme Court justice (or any judge for that matter) is to interpret the Constitution and statutes fairly, following a consistent approach we call due process. The judiciary is not empowered as an unelected, independent body that legislates, writes or otherwise creates new laws. Its role is not to read anything into the Constitution, or to read anything into any law which is not already in it.

To illustrate, in *King v. Burwell (2015)*, the Supreme Court decided that tax credits to subsidize certain purchases of health insurance can be given if purchased on an Exchange established by a State or the Federal government. The problem with this decision is that the Patient Protection and Affordable Care Act clearly and unequivocally states that the tax credit subsidies only apply to insurance purchases made on State Exchanges. Justice Scalia writes in his dissenting opinion about the majority opinion of the Court with these words:

> The Court holds that when the Patient Protection and Affordable Care Act says "Exchange established by the State" it means "Exchange established by the State or Federal Government." That is of course quite absurd, and the Court's 21 pages of explanation make it no less so.[94]

Then, he goes on to say:

> Words no longer have meaning if an Exchange that is not established by a State is "established by the State."[95]

It would appear that the Supreme Court made a political decision to keep the Affordable Care Act afloat by allowing subsidies to insurance purchased on Exchanges established by the Federal government. Without question, the words of Congress in the law are clear and concise. Congress chose to limit subsidies to *Exchanges established by the States*, not established by the Federal government. The Supreme Court overturned the will of the people as determined in this case by Congress, elected by the people.

In a second example of recent aggressive judicial activism on the part of the Supreme Court, there is the case of *Obergefell v. Hodges (2015)* that deals with same-sex marriage. The Constitution does not mention marriage. It leaves any legislation regarding marriage presumably to the States. In *Obergefell v. Hodges*, the Supreme Court decided that States must license a marriage between two people of the same sex.[96] Leaving aside for now the morality and the desirability of same-sex marriage and strictly viewing it from a Constitutional perspective, this decision has no Constitutional basis.

It appears the Supreme Court has now set up a precedent that permits nine unelected justices to read anything they choose into the Constitution. Will they decide to find a right to polyamory in the Constitution next? Perhaps, they will see a right to prostitution in our Founding Document.

Following the *Obergefell v. Hodges* decision, Justice Alito in a media interview suggested other ramifications of this judicial activism. For example, possibly the Supreme Court will say the minimum wage is unconstitutional because it violates the right of a business owner to pay what he wants to pay an employee. Or, progressive justices might decide the Constitution guarantees all citizens a free annual income from the Federal government. They might even decide the Constitution provides a right to a free college education.[97]

If the Supreme Court can literally read anything into the Constitution they want, there is no limit to their power and ultimately, there is no Rule of Law. It's all arbitrary, a judicial dictatorship that is more powerful than the Congress or the president.

Once again in *Obergefell v. Hodges*, the Supreme Court took on the role of a legislature. It issued a court decision that was truly a social policy decision that more appropriately should have been determined in State legislatures. It ignored the Constitution and neglected its obligation to decide cases based on the Constitution and statutes, following the Rule of Law. It was an Anti-Constitutional action.

Second, let's look at some presidential actions that appear to be plainly Anti-Constitutional in nature. Consider the Iran nuclear deal agreed to by the United States, five other global powers, and Iran in July 2015.[98] Rather than following the Constitution in Article 2 Section 2 which requires two-thirds of the Senate to approve a treaty with foreign nations, the president by-passed Congress by formulating the Iran nuclear deal as an Executive Agreement.[99] It appears to be a masked and covert Anti-Constitutional action.

In addition, the president's administration has fostered lawlessness by unilaterally waiving, delaying, or ignoring ObamaCare provisions without Congressional authorization. The president has sometimes even decreed specific rulings in press conferences, flaunting Congress publically and defying Congressional intentions. Moreover, these unilateral decisions to waive, delay or ignore parts of that law have taken place not once, not twice, but literally dozens of times.[100]

In a further illustration, the president's administration appears to have used the Internal Revenue Service (IRS) directly against its own political adversaries to thwart their ability to obtain tax-exempt status.[101] If true, these political actions seem to fly in the face of our political freedom of speech. Clearly, they would be an abuse of power. Indeed, using the power of the Federal government in such a manner, smacks of dictatorship and is certainly a blatant disregard for the Rule of Law in a democracy. Once again, it appears to be more Anti-Constitutional actions on the part of the president's administration.

One final blatant example of lawlessness and Anti-Constitutional behavior on the part of the executive branch is the disregard for the nation's immigration laws as well as the deliberate release of illegal immigrants, who have committed felonies, back into the general population. Releasing criminals back into the American population, rather than deporting them, not only ignores common sense, but it puts Americans at risk of future crimes.[102]

Americans are genuinely living through a period of extensive attacks on our Constitution. It's definitely the Anti-Constitutional Era.

Prediction #1

Approaching the 2016 presidential election, America's moral outrage from coast-to-coast, from Alaska to Hawaii, and across the continental United States is enormous. It's pulsating. It's ready to deal Washington insiders, the consultant class, well-known politicians of the baby boomer generation, the Republican Party, the Democratic Party, and the mainstream media some stunning surprises. This book will forecast those upcoming shocks and their resulting shockwaves.

Prediction #1. The critical presidential election of 2016 will usher in a new American Constitutional Era. It will be called the Conservative Era and will feature a return to America's traditional principles of government based on morality and freedom. It will be characterized by a return to upholding the Constitution and the Rule of Law.

The Conservative Era is described in the next chapter.

Chapter 2

Current Events and the Reasons for the New Conservative Era

While some nations experience change through bullets and violent revolutions, America has a history of dealing with the need for change through ballots and peaceful political realignments. More specifically, when American voters sense the moral principles articulated in the Declaration of Independence and the political principles encapsulated in the Constitution are being overlooked, or disregarded, or ignored, or flagrantly abused, Americans develop a sense of moral outrage. If, over a period of several elections, politicians, political parties and political institutions don't react and respond to the voter outrage adequately, citizens will take action with their ballots.

In other words, if the government doesn't mend its ways, the voters will hold the politicians in office accountable. America has always been a "government of the people, by the people, for the people" as Abraham Lincoln profoundly stated in his Gettysburg Address on November 19, 1863.[103]

Indeed, when the moral outrage of Americans reaches a crescendo of disappointment, frustration and anger with the government, the moral outrage results in an electoral tipping point. Voters will make a normally recurring presidential election into a relatively rare, critical presidential election.

High voter turnout is one characteristic of some critical presidential elections. Other characteristics of a critical presidential election include changes in political leadership, changes in the dominant political parties holding office, political party realignments, and political institution realignments.

Closely associated with some critical presidential elections is also the creation of a new communications media and its growing influence on voters.[104] It seems that a new political communications media is able to empower and to focus the moral outrage of voters on the issues facing the nation and to create a channel through which the moral outrage can be directed toward the political institutions.

One example of a political communications media with an impact on America is the role of the "pamphlet," quite possibly the most powerful political communications device in revolutionary America.

Another example is the newspaper. As a political communications media, it had a big impact on the critical presidential election of 1828. In the early years of the Jacksonian Era, newspaper circulation was about one million, a number that roughly quadrupled from the newspaper circulation at the time of the previous critical election of 1800.[105] That's a big jump in potential political impact.

During the Progressive Era, the mass circulation press brought political information to citizens living in the larger cities. Names like William Randolph Hearst, Edward Scripps and Joseph Pulitzer might come to mind for those who are familiar with the history of publishing. The Progressive Era is associated with newspapers that had large urban circulations, as well as with popular magazines.[106]

Of course, television was thrust onto the political scene with the Kennedy-Nixon debates in 1960. Some believe it was responsible for Kennedy's narrow victory over Nixon. Kennedy's youthful appearance outshined Nixon's dour look under the powerful lens of the TV camera.[107] Subsequently, however, TV came into its own in a commanding manner during the beginning of the Entitlement Era. Recall, for example, the highly charged "Daisy" ad that counted down to a nuclear explosion, used against Barry Goldwater during the critical presidential election of 1964.[108]

During a critical presidential election, sometimes political parties will change the planks in their platforms. Sometimes, political parties will change their political philosophies. Sometimes, political parties will change their names. Still at other times, new or greatly modified parties will emerge from the remnants of the previous American Constitutional Era.

Often, the newly realigned and reconstituted parties will find that their core constituencies have dramatically been altered beyond previous expectations. Support for both major parties might come from different geographical regions, or distinct economic groups, or dissimilar social segments. Major shifts are common in critical presidential elections and their aftermath.

In parallel to political party realignments, we also see political institution realignments. For example, after a critical presidential election, we expect to see a movement in the judicial philosophy of the Supreme Court over time. After such an election, as normal attrition in the ranks of the justices take place, room is made for new presidential appointments. This permits the results of the recent critical presidential election to reverberate throughout the Supreme Court as well as throughout the entire Federal judicial system. Similarly, we expect to see presidential appointments to Federal agencies and their regulatory apparatus to gradually and ultimately reflect the results of the election.

The critical presidential election of 2016 will be the pivot point from the old Anti-Constitutional Era to a new American Constitutional Era, the forthcoming Conservative Era.

What is Fueling the Moral Outrage of Americans and the New Conservative Era?

As America proceeds to the critical presidential election of 2016, it does so in a climate of great crisis, fear and intrepidation. Americans sense a grave Constitutional crisis on the horizon. Many Americans believe our liberty protected for 240 years by the Constitution is literally hanging on by a thread. They see their freedoms curtailed nearly everywhere they turn. The regulatory state virtually circumscribes their every action, their every move, and even their very lives by intimately controlling the healthcare system that controls access to their medical care.

Violating the Constitution and the Bill of Rights. But, even more than stifling regulations, Americans sense they are losing the basic freedoms contained in the Bill of Rights. Freedom of Speech in schools, in colleges and universities, at work, and in the public square are tightly controlled by the progressive socialist forces of political correctness. Americans can be thrown out of school; or lose their jobs, careers and livelihoods; or be shunned in social situations; simply for expressing a conservative opinion.

It closely parallels the cultural climate of Nazi Germany before World War II in which politically compliant thought and action were mandated across institutions large and small.[109] The reason for imposing such political correctness by the forces of progressive socialists on America today is simply that socialism requires all citizens to agree with progressive elites. Without complete cooperation, it's difficult to control the nation.

Incidentally, two victims of the politically correct, progressive socialist mindset are truth and morality. Progressives constantly must bend the truth (more precisely, must lie outright) and forego morality (for example, break the Rule of Law and create a climate of lawlessness) in order to superimpose their power over cultural, political and economic forces and institutions in America.[110]

Plus, this vise grip on Freedom of Speech impacts not only everyday workers, but goes all the way up to the highest levels of corporations and other organizations.

Surprisingly, in something as straight forward as affirming marriage as a profoundly, wonderful institution between a man and woman for the purpose of mutual love and for the purpose of having, loving and nurturing children, Americans can now be harassed for holding onto their traditional views of the definition of marriage. This is hard to believe since the definition of marriage has withstood the test of time for thousands of years, throughout nearly every civilization known to exist.

In the minds of progressive socialists and their totalitarian political correctness, how is it possible that Freedom of Speech with regard to the issue of same-sex marriage might be lost so quickly? Why do some progressives close their minds to all but their own narrow-minded thinking? With progressive socialists, the answer always seems to be power. Power for socialists is more important to them than freedom for everyone else.

In addition to encroachments on their Freedom of Speech, Americans recognize their Second Amendment rights to keep and bear arms are being curtailed progressively with an incrementally tightening of sundry rules and regulations. In cities across the nation, gun control laws fail to avert violence. In effect, they seem to encourage violence by criminals who feel able to prey on unarmed citizens.[111]

It's true, where gun control laws exist, only criminals have guns. In those places with gun control laws, ordinary citizens often feel unprotected. Crime rates can often soar. Law-abiding citizens are restricted from owning guns for their own protection. When citizens are free to own guns, crime rates decline or at the very least don't increase. Studies confirm these consistent conclusions.[112]

Why should a senior citizen relinquish the right to own a gun because they have chosen a relative or friend to manage their Social Security income and other financial affairs? Such a ban is apparently under development by the administration.[113] Does having a son or daughter pay their bills every month imply a senior is mentally ill or violent? Or, does it imply that a senior citizen doesn't require protection from inner city crime in an older urban neighborhood?

Let's face it. Progressive socialists don't want citizens to keep and bear arms. For them, the Second Amendment is just another roadblock to their totalitarian, progressive socialist utopia (or so they seem to think).

The research data are clear. Locations that outlaw guns are the same places that crime rates are typically higher. Locations that permit law-abiding citizens to own guns are the safer locations that normally experience lower crime rates. The growing body of evidence appears to be consistent and the obvious research conclusions seem to be irrefutable.[114]

The list of attacks on the Bill of Rights continues across America. Americans are justified in their concern for our loss of freedom prior to the critical presidential election of 2016.

Violating the Separation of Powers. Adding to the angst of Americans as we approach the 2016 presidential election are the actions of the current president and his administration. Americans see a current president that flaunts the Constitution and appears to put himself above the other two branches of the Federal government (unless in some cases, the other branches happen to acquiesce to, or agree with, him on certain issues).

The principle of separation of powers (among the legislative, executive and judicial branches of the Federal government) is essential to the effective protection of liberty within America. The Constitution has never been at such an enormous risk of being completely enervated through the accumulation and consolidation of legislative, executive and judicial powers in the hands of the president.

Independently, but nevertheless of great importance, an unchecked Supreme Court creating new laws where none exist, also violates the separation of powers. Americans are concerned with a number of high visibility incursions of the Supreme Court into legislating political policies that should be left to the States or to the people. The previous chapter mentions the *King v. Burwell (2015)* decision and the *Obergefell v. Hodges (2015)* decision as two recent egregious and unconstitutional encroachments on legislative power by the Supreme Court.

In Federalist No. 47, James Madison captures the critical importance of the separation of powers in these salient words:

> The accumulation of all powers, legislative, executive, and judiciary, in the same hands, whether of one, a few, or many, and whether hereditary, self-appointed, or elective, may justly be pronounced the very definition of tyranny.[115]

America wants the Constitution to be followed. The separation of powers is required to guarantee America's freedom.

Violating the Rule of Law. In addition to the attacks on the Bill of Rights and the breakdown in the separation of powers, there is a third critical reason for the grave Constitutional crisis Americans sense entering into the 2016 critical presidential election. This is the flagrant disregard for the Rule of Law.

Just as the Bill of Rights coming under constant attack and the separation of powers being whittled away are both clear violations of the Constitution, a more general attack is taking place on the Rule of Law across America. Parenthetically, it's worth noting that an attack on the Rule of Law actually encompasses attacks on both Constitutional law and attacks on specific statutes. They are broken out into two distinct categories here just to emphasize the importance of the direct assault on the Constitution itself, which protects all of our liberties.

In the previous chapter, a few examples of attacks on the Rule of Law were cited. One example was the highly questionable IRS actions apparently blocking conservative groups from obtaining tax-exempt status. A second illustration already mentioned is the open disregard for our immigration laws that should be enforced to protect America's borders from the inflow of illegal immigrants.

In addition to these examples, sometimes inappropriate and excessive enforcement of the Rule of Law can take place for seemingly political purposes. One case in point was the government prosecution of Wisconsin conservatives. This is an apparent egregious illustration of prosecutorial abuse.[116]

In this instance, conservative non-profit groups in Wisconsin were investigated for apparently doing no more than speaking out about State government and issues before the State legislature. According to one authority:

> The prosecutors treated the targets of their investigation as if they were the members of a dangerous drug cartel or mob operation. As the Wisconsin Supreme Court said, they

executed search warrants against the personal homes and families of the leaders of these nonprofits in "pre-dawn, armed, paramilitary-style raids in which bright floodlights were used to illuminate the targets' homes."

This was dangerous, unjustified, and unnecessary unless, of course, the intent was to intimidate conservatives and punish them for speaking up.[117]

Certainly, this is not the way to use the police powers. Fortunately, the Wisconsin Supreme Court decided to put an end to this investigation that flaunted the Rule of Law.[118] But, the fact that this even occurred in America is deeply disturbing.

Providing more illustrations, John Fund and Hans von Spakovsky document the attack on the Rule of Law and the politicization of law enforcement within the Department of Justice (DOJ). They cite many troubling examples at DOJ.[119] More information related to attacks on the Rule of Law and the related issues of lawlessness and overcriminalization are also available in my book *Renewing America and Its Heritage of Freedom*.[120]

Space doesn't permit delving into more depth on this topic here. But, it can be said that there exists a true lack of equality under the Rule of Law, leading up to the critical presidential election of 2016. Furthermore, this overt attack on the Rule of Law is currently plaguing America as a direct result of progressive socialist thoughts, policies and actions.

Two special cases involving the attack on the Rule of Law deal with violating the domestic peace. This is obviously an important concern of Americans, who expect to live in peace at home and in their neighborhoods. The first of these two special cases concerns urban rioting and racial tensions, while the second special case involves a national crime wave that America is experiencing prior to the presidential election of 2016.

Violating Domestic Peace – Rioting and Racial Tensions in Our Cities. Besides the problem with not maintaining equality under the Rule of Law, urban rioting presents still another area that illustrates the breakdown of law and order, and the attack on the Rule of Law.

In fact, in the arena of urban rioting, some progressive politicians seem to believe that it's acceptable to permit some citizens to vent their frustrations in highly-charged demonstrations that risk escalating into urban rioting. These same progressive politicians can even go as far as ordering the National Guard to stand-down from law enforcement protection in volatile situations, potentially risking death and injuries, as well as extensive and wanton private property damage to law-abiding citizens.[121]

Riots in Ferguson, Missouri[122] and Baltimore, Maryland[123] in 2015 raise concerns for many Americans. Urban rioting is actually another clear violation of the Rule of Law, especially if it's not dealt with as expeditiously as possible.

Violating Domestic Peace – A National Crime Wave. Closely related to urban rioting is a nationwide crime wave. Of course, it's a form of lawlessness too. Consider these examples.

Baltimore experienced 32 shootings over the 2015 Memorial Day weekend, with the month of May (at that time) being the city's most violent month in 15 years.[124] Heather Mac Donald further reports these 2015 statistics:

> In Milwaukee, homicides were up 180% by May 17 over the same period the previous year. Through April, shootings in St. Louis were up 39%, robberies 43%, and homicides 25%.
> …
> Murders in Atlanta were up 32% as of mid-May. Shootings in Chicago had increased 24% and homicides 17%.
> Shootings and other violent felonies in Los Angeles had spiked by 25%; in New York, murder was up nearly 13%, and gun violence 7%.
>
> Those citywide statistics from law-enforcement officials mask even more startling neighborhood-level increases. Shooting incidents are up 500% in an East Harlem precinct compared with last year; in a South Central Los Angeles

police division, shooting victims are up 100%. [125]

The nationwide crime wave traces its current origins in part to the same faulty progressive socialist policies that blame the police with racial bias first.[126] Rather than blaming the actual lawbreakers first, progressives seem to blame the police first. However, look at Baltimore as an example. Racial diversity in Baltimore (where 40% of the police officers are black) didn't avoid the unfortunate tragedy of Freddie Gray's death in police custody. Recall that his death was the assumed proximate cause of the 2015 Baltimore riots.[127]

What's the faulty logic behind blaming the police first? Progressive socialists seem to feel that frustration among blacks is understandable due to long-standing racial bias in their communities and rampant social problems. They believe what is needed are more social programs in the inner cities, and more spending on inner city programs, not stricter law enforcement.[128] Progressive politicians apparently fail to recognize the critical need for maintaining the Rule of Law as a fundamental building block of a peaceful and prosperous nation.

Indeed, if we want to help the poor lift themselves out of poverty and not be permanently dependent on government handouts, we must start by making their cities, towns and neighborhoods peaceful. Without the Rule of Law, prosperity is only wishful thinking. If a black teenager can't make it to work safely due to the threat of crimes and violence in an inner city neighborhood, how can he or she hold down a steady job or even travel to and from school to get educated?

Potential new job-creating businesses also might hesitate to open a new business in an area where there is high crime. Law enforcement is vital to every neighborhood, including poor inner city areas. Who is hurt the most when entrepreneurs and small business owners refuse to open new businesses in a high crime area? The residents who won't get the jobs the businesses will offer, and the citizens who won't have access to the goods and services the businesses bring to the neighborhoods being served.

Progressive socialists also apparently fail to see that their social policies and programs are the root cause of much of the heartache and social anguish experienced by minorities and the urban poor. Not only is government-dependency a handicap for true economic advancement for these individuals, but the costs of such programs remove dollars from the private sector than can generate new jobs, new businesses, new opportunities, and new economic growth. Rather than create growth within the private sector, progressives like to funnel tax dollars into failing government programs that create more problems than they solve.

Americans don't condone urban rioting, urban crime, lawlessness and ignoring the Rule of Law. Instead, Americans support their police departments and county sheriffs in general, and want and expect that the laws will be enforced as they should be enforced. Americans would much prefer the urban poor and in fact, all individuals, to be law-abiding, financially independent, self-supporting and economically successful citizens.

Putting all of above factors and examples together, it's completely understandable why Americans sense the Constitution and the Bill of Rights are under dangerous attack, why the separation of powers is under heavy assault, and why the Rule of Law is under devastating attack. It all adds up to America's sense of deep concern and grave crisis. Plus, it all helps explain America's strong moral outrage at this time in our history and America's frustration at the political parties that have not addressed their moral outrage after a number of election cycles.

These issues of morality and freedom are not the only challenges facing America today. Palpable threats to national security and economic security are fanning the flames of moral outrage as well, setting the stage for the critical presidential election of 2016 and the subsequent, new Conservative Era.

What are the National Security Issues adding to the Moral Outrage of Americans?

Further fueling the grave national crisis that Americans sense today are issues surrounding our national security and economic security. Any one of these issues by itself would likely not trigger a critical presidential election, let alone a new American Constitutional Era. However, these additional issues, when taken together with the enormous moral outrage that already exists over issues of morality and freedom, increase the energy and drive for major political change in America. Indeed, all these issues of morality and freedom, national security and economic security are sufficient to propel us toward the critical presidential election in 2016 and the dawning of the new Conservative Era.

Let's look at these additional national security and economic security threats that are making American voters frustrated, angry and upset.

The Threats Posed by America's Unprotected Borders and Illegal Immigration. These threats include: (1) terrorists, drug lords and violent criminals; (2) diseases and epidemics; and (3) real economic burdens imposed on our healthcare, welfare, education and criminal justice systems.

Americans do worry considerably about an on-going influx of illegal immigrants that include not only millions of the poor and uneducated from Mexico and Central America, but also the threat that some illegal immigrants are actually violent criminals, dangerous drug lords, or anti-American, Middle East terrorists. With a porous border on our southern flank, ISIS and other terrorists have the ability to slip their soldiers across our border and into our cities and towns.

One news source reports that drug cartels armed with AK-47's control parts of American territory only about 30 miles from Phoenix.[129] That's both astonishing and extremely disturbing for Americans to learn. If that's not bad enough, there is no movement on the part of the Federal government to reclaim this territory and bring it back under American control. How can America allow drug lords to control our sovereign territory? Is it any wonder why Americans sense a grave national crisis as we approach the 2016 presidential election?

Fox News reported recently that a self-described jihadist said that ISIS has 71 trained soldiers in the United States in 15 States ready to carry out operations against America. The unsettling threat went so far as to name five of the 15 States that were said to have ISIS soldiers: Virginia, Maryland, Illinois, California, and Michigan.[130] Once again, this is a potentially alarming warning and indicates that we need to close our borders to protect our national security. Americans are justified in their deep concern for avoiding deaths, injuries and private property damage.

Americans are also concerned that some illegal immigrants might be carrying virulent diseases into America as well. Consider some health related information about Central America, the source of many illegal immigrants flowing into America.

Around 183,000 cases of chikungunya ("the virus of pain") were reported in Central America in 2014. Like Dengue Fever and Yellow Fever, it's carried by mosquitoes. At the time, there was also a major epidemic of Dengue Fever going on in Honduras, Guatemala, and El Salvador with a staggering 120,000 cases and at least 60 deaths. In addition, better known diseases such as tuberculosis have had infections rates approximately ten times higher in Central America than in the United States.[131]

It seems foolish to allow our southern borders to be open to illegal immigrants who might be ill and who might bring infections and diseases into America. It is simple common sense to protect American citizens from diseases and epidemics.

Besides the obvious national security threats just mentioned, there are the economic burdens placed on our healthcare, welfare and education systems by illegal immigrants. One estimate from the Heritage Foundation is that illegal immigrants cost the government $60 billion annually in net benefits, over and above, any possible taxes illegal immigrants might pay.[132]

While Americans are a generous people, rushing to the aid of other people around the world, who are the victims of natural disasters, America's healthcare, welfare, education, and criminal justice systems are limited in scope and capacity. Some believe that America should allow in all immigrants from around the world. But, that is an economic impossibility. Economic resources are always limited. In fact, an "economic" resource is a scarce resource. Otherwise, we wouldn't need to be as concerned with the study of economics at all.

Open borders imply access for an unlimited number of illegal immigrants to the economic resources of America. Do the progressive socialist supporters of unlimited, illegal immigration propose we allow 10 million more illegal immigrants into America? Or, do they propose we allow 100 million more illegal immigrants into America? Or, do they propose we allow 1 billion more illegal immigrants into America? Or, do they propose we allow 7 billion more illegal immigrants into America?

What is their limit on the number of illegal immigrants that our healthcare, welfare, education and criminal justice systems should absorb and accommodate? More importantly, how do these progressive socialist proponents of open borders and illegal immigration propose we pay for it? Do they think America should borrow the money from China? From Russia? From Iran? From Greece – a welfare State struggling from its own progressive socialist policies and programs? Plus, how do they propose we pay the interest on this additional national debt every year?

It's true. Americans are justifiably frustrated, angry and upset that our current administration refuses to close our borders to the real threats posed by Illegal Immigration, namely, terrorists, drug lords, violent criminals, diseases, potential epidemics and the obvious economic burdens imposed on our healthcare, welfare, education and criminal justice systems.

The Threats Posed by Potential Terrorist Attacks. These threats include: (1) terrorist shootings, beheadings, bombings; (2) laser weapons directed against commercial airliners; and (3) drone attacks against people, commercial airliners and other private property.

In addition to all the threats associated with illegal immigration, Americans fret that our homeland is no longer secure from terrorist shootings, beheadings, bombings, and other terrorist attacks. Regardless of whether the Federal government allows terrorists to slip across the borders illegally, or invites large numbers of potential immigrants in legally through the legal immigration system, the threats are real.

We need to address some key concerns. For example, are we adequately screening legal immigrants for terrorist connections, or terrorist ties, or terrorist leanings? Have we assessed the probability that new legal immigrants are genuinely seeking freedom and opportunity in America, or are secretly plotting jihad when they arrive in America?

Does America really need to distribute about one million green cards annually to new legal immigrants? Plus, how should we distribute green cards among all the many immigrants hoping to migrate to America from all the different countries from around the world whose citizens seek to live in America?

Is it time to take a break, a moratorium for a few years, and assess whether the current legal immigration system is working in the best interests of America? Should we make changes? If so, what changes should we make?

Indeed, Americans worry that terrorist shootings, beheadings, bombings and other attacks will occur and will increase in frequency and severity over time. To Americans, these threats are growing and our government is largely ignoring the threats. Data support the electorate's fears and concerns. Let's look at a few examples.

On July 4, 2015, a potential terrorist was arrested by law enforcement for weapons violations. That was fortunate because this particular potential terrorist was building pressure cooker bombs from pressure cookers purchased at Walmart. He was also involved in making Molotov cocktails. His plans included using them at a college or college bar, grabbing hostages, and possibly executing them and showing the actual executions live over the Internet.[133]

The July 4th 2015 potential terrorist was a supporter of ISIS and viewed America as the enemy of "faith." According to the Heritage

Foundation, this thwarted potential attack is labelled as terrorist plot #72, the 72nd Islamist terror plot on the American homeland since 9/11.[134]

Contributing to concerns about potential terrorism include these two reports on the Transportation Security Administration (TSA). According to the Department of Homeland Security's Inspector General's office, 73 airline industry employees with terrorism-related activity codes were able to slip through TSA security clearances. This worrisome report was in addition to another report that TSA failed to detect mock explosives and weapons 95% of the time when tested by undercover agents.[135] Not a very reassuring statistic for the flying public. So, from these reports, we learn that some airline employees might be terrorists and TSA doesn't always locate mock explosives and weapons.

Another example might appear to be terrorist related (or possibly terrorist inspired), but officials didn't appear to have evidence at the time of the incident to make a definitive connection to terrorism. In this case, a man savagely beheaded a woman at a food plant and also stabbed a second woman in Moore, Oklahoma. The man was said to be a recent convert to Islam who had been fired from the food plant the day before the incident.[136] A local police department spokesperson was quoted in *The New York Times* as saying the man: "recently started trying to convert some of his co-workers to the Muslim religion."[137]

It's not known if it was a terrorist attack, a terrorist inspired attack, or simply a disgruntled ex-employee who vented his frustrations in workplace related violence. But, the violent beheading seems characteristic of other ISIS violence reported in the media.

Clearly, potential terrorist attacks or terrorist looking attacks are going on in America. While a rock solid nexus can't always be proven, a terrorist signature seems quite apparent in many of these acts of violence.

Take the recent shootings of military personnel in Chattanooga, Tennessee. Four marines and one sailor were shot and killed by a man born in Kuwait and living in the United States. A police officer was also shot, but fortunately was expected to survive.[138] According to Fox News, "known ISIS-affiliated Twitter accounts were celebrating the attack, which comes at the end of Ramadan."[139]

At the time of this incident, no terrorist connection was officially made public. But, do the facts that the attacks were against American military personnel, made by a person born in the Middle East, and celebrated by ISIS-affiliated accounts on social media indicate that this was truly a terrorist attack?

Terrorism is perpetrated much like guerilla warfare. It's more stealth and the soldiers are not always easy to identify. While Americans might not know for sure if any given attack is a terrorist attack, these attacks add to their overall sense of fear and concern. Americans are not used to hearing about beheadings in the workplace or military personnel being killed in a recruitment center or on military bases in the United States. This violence is new to Americans and it is adding to their moral outrage about what's happening to America.

Indeed, how many are terrorists from overseas have sneaked across our open border on the south? Plus, how many legal immigrants from the Middle East have come to America and now see their role as participants in global jihad against our nation? Regrettably, we don't know the answers to these vital questions, and our government seems to downplay the palpable threat of homeland terrorism.

Consider two final potential terrorist threats that concern some Americans.

Laser targeting of commercial airliners is a growing and real concern for Americans too. We now know that there have been literally thousands of such potentially deadly attacks in America's skies. CNN reported that in August 2015 over the skies of New Jersey there were 12 laser incidents with commercial airliners in one night alone. According to the FAA, all told for the year 2014, there were a remarkable 3,894 laser attacks.[140]

The impact of such attacks can be damaging to pilots, potentially burning a pilot's cornea. In addition, brightly illuminating the cockpit of a jet at night can disorient and distract pilots during critical takeoff and landing maneuvers.[141] Laser attacks are certainly a threat to the flying public.

The rising use of drones might become a favored technology adopted by terrorists too. There appears to be a high probability that armed or weaponized drones will be available to most governments within a decade or so. With this widespread availability likely to occur in the near future and the known state sponsorship of terrorist groups by some countries, armed drones can be expected to be used by terrorists as well.[142]

Even non-weaponized drones might potentially cause a mid-air disaster by purposely running into a targeted commercial jetliner. ABC News reported that:

> The Federal Aviation Administration said in a statement that it was investigating a report of an unmanned aircraft being operated illegally near LaGuardia Airport around 11 a.m. today as a plane prepared to land. The crew of Shuttle America Flight 2708 said it had to climb 200 feet to "avoid" the aircraft as the plane traveled over Brooklyn at an altitude of 2,700 feet, officials said.[143]

Drones are a growing concern and a likely mechanism for future potential terrorist attacks against America.

Besides the threats posed by illegal immigration and the threats posed by terrorist attacks, let's turn next to the third major set of national security threats adding to America's moral outrage preceding the critical presidential election of 2016. These are the threats posed to America's national security by the one-sided, bad Iran nuclear deal formulated as an executive agreement by the current administration, rather than as a standard U. S. treaty subject to a two-thirds approval vote in the Senate.

The Threats Posed by the Terrible Iran Nuclear Deal. These threats include: (1) Iran will probably get nuclear weapons, ballistic missiles and other military weapons; (2) Iran will probably get money from the elimination of economic sanctions for funding terrorism; (3) Iran will probably get to keep American hostages; and (4) Iran will probably get self-verification of military sites (not 24 x 7 x any site inspections).

In another area of deep concern for Americans is the badly constructed Iran nuclear deal made by the current administration. It further risks America's safety and security. This deal all but assures Iran will get a nuclear weapon.

The Iran nuclear deal is an effectively unilateral agreement that provides Iran with tremendous military and economic advantages with little, if any, real substantive value to the United States and its national security. In reality, this deal is more likely to damage America's national security, its national security interests, and the national security of its long-time ally Israel.

Consider some of the benefits to Iran. First, Iran gets a glide path to nuclear weapons if they choose to pursue them (which is highly probable and to be expected).

Next, Iran's ballistic missile program is not prohibited, is not inhibited, and instead, is allowed and fostered by this deal, by not requiring that the U. N. embargo resolution against ballistic missile material or technology to be continued. In a similar manner, the Iran nuclear deal doesn't require the extension of the corresponding U. N. arms embargo as well. This bad Iran nuclear deal doesn't prohibit either of these two U. N. embargo resolutions from being terminated.[144]

According to an op-ed piece in *The Wall Street Journal*:

> The current embargo was implemented by two resolutions: No. 1696 (2006) and No. 1929 (2010). The first bars the sale or transfer to Iran of any material or technology that might be useful to a ballistic-missile program, and the second does the same for "battle tanks, armored combat vehicles, large caliber artillery systems, combat aircraft, attack helicopters, warships, missiles, or missile systems."[145]

Since the Iran nuclear deal, the U. N. Security Council has adopted resolution No. 2231 (2015) endorsing the Iran nuclear deal and apparently calling for the termination of both the 1696 and 1929 resolutions subject to verification of Iranian compliance.[146] Of course, this means the opening up of the possibility of Iran obtaining both ballistic missile technology and an assortment of military equipment; thereby,   enhancing Iran's military strength and empowering its ability to fund and control further terrorist activities against America and Israel.

Iran will also receive a "signing bonus" of sorts of $50 billion in economic sanctions relief and the additional unfreezing of about $150 billion in frozen assets.[147] In addition, it will receive still more revenues from the sale of its oil resources.[148] All of these economic revenues will flow into Iran, a nation that our State Department lists as a "State Sponsor of Terrorism."[149] It would be naïve to expect these resources will not be utilized by Iran to foment more terrorism in the world.

The Iran nuclear deal also doesn't include a provision for releasing American hostages and prisoners in Iran. A hostage release gesture should be a given for Iran if it were truly a nation operating in good faith within the global community of nations. It should also have been expected and demanded by the U. S. government prior to signing this one-sided deal.

Finally, the terrible Iran nuclear deal comes with an apparent secret "side deal" that allows for Iranian self-inspection and self-verification of its compliance with the agreement.[150] A much safer approach obviously would be for the U. S. to have 24 x 7 x 365, on-site, any-site, inspection privileges without prior notifications of impending inspections.

Even the current deal (without the secret side deal) effectively leaves some sites totally off limits. In particular, the Parchin military facility where prior nuclear arms work was done is conspicuously absent from the deal.[151] In addition, the current deal requires a long gap between notice to Iran for an inspection request and the actual in-person inspection.[152] Of course, with the self-verification protocol announced after the deal closed, the question of inspections is moot. Iran gets to certify its own compliance with the nuclear deal. It's certainly understandable why Americans gain no comfort from such an incredible self-inspection regime.

Many Americans believe that this deal makes no sense for America's national security and that it might more easily draw us into a war in the Middle East.[153] Plus, it fosters the possibility of a regional arms race in the Middle East as well.[154] Further, it gives Iran clear access to nuclear weapons that might be shared with Iran's terrorist clients. These nuclear weapons might be used against Israel, and might even be deployed against America in an Electro-Magnetic Pulse (EMP) attack as discussed in the next sub-section below.

This is a terrible deal for America and adds more fuel to America's moral outrage over how our nation is currently being misled with a progressive socialist philosophy that ignores or minimizes America's vital national security and interests.

Let's turn our attention to the fourth set of national security threats that are causing America's moral outrage before the critical presidential election of 2016.

The Threats Posed by a Potential Electro-Magnetic Pulse (EMP) Attack on America and the Meltdown of America's Electric Grid. An Electro-Magnetic Pulse (EMP) attack requires two primary components: a nuclear weapon and a delivery platform such as a ballistic missile. To create an EMP attack, a nuclear weapon is detonated in the sky above a nation. It might be 200 miles high. The height can vary. The function of the ballistic missile is to launch the nuclear weapon and place it in the appropriate location for the planned nuclear explosion.[155]

The bad Iran nuclear deal facilitates Iran obtaining both nuclear weapons and ballistic missiles. As a result, this State Department designated state sponsor of terrorism will probably have the means to carry out EMP attacks against the United States. Is an EMP attack something America should protect itself from? Is it really a big deal?

Yes, an EMP attack is unquestionably a big deal. An EMP attack is unthinkable. Its potential devastation is incredible. Its impact on American civilization would be deadly and its aftermath would last for literally months, years, or possibly decades.[156] Quite literally, such an EMP attack can shut down America's electric utility grid in less than one second after a nuclear weapon detonates over the United States. The ramifications from the destruction of America's electric grid will cripple the nation.[157]

With the loss of America's electric grid and electricity, military and civilian damage would be unprecedented and staggering.[158] Communications, electronics, banking, transportation, refrigeration, food production and distribution would probably be largely wiped out. Chaos and anarchy would be widespread. Police and emergency communications equipment would be knocked out. Tens of millions of Americans would die from the lack of food and water and the lack of critical medical supplies and healthcare capabilities.[159]

One estimate of casualties by U. S. analyst Peter Vincent Fry is that up to 90% of Americans might die as a result of an EMP attack.[160] Even if he is over-estimating the death toll, casualties will be a major blow to the nation on a level never before experienced.

In fact, the threat of a potential EMP attack is the reason that the North American Aerospace Defense Command (NORAD) decided to move back into its cold war Cheyenne Mountain headquarters near Colorado Springs, Colorado. Cheyenne Mountain is hardened against an EMP attack.[161]

Of course, in the hands of our allies, nuclear capabilities and ballistic missile technology are not likely to threaten us, and are reasonably safe. But, the Iran situation is particularly troubling. After all, American military officials have translated a secret Iranian military textbook that endorses an EMP attack on the United States. Apparently, 20 specific locations over the U. S. have been targeted already.[162]

This is the same nation that has demonstrations with citizens shouting "Death to America" and calling for the destruction of our ally, Israel.[163]

One news source in 2015 quotes Hossein Salami, the Commander of the Iranian Revolutionary Guard Corps, as saying: "we welcome war with the U.S."[164] Are these the words of an ally?

Should America put Iran on a glide path to nuclear weapons and ballistic missiles? Should America help Iran get the means to launch an EMP attack against the United States?

Remember, this is the same country that is a state sponsor of terrorism. Iran might also choose to give any newly developed nuclear weapons or ballistic missiles to one of their client terrorist groups. These terrorist organizations might then perpetrate an EMP attack on America.

The threats posed by a potential Electro-Magnetic Pulse (EMP) attack on America and the immediate meltdown of America's electric grid are serious. Americans are justified in their deep concerns for our national security in the area of protecting our nation from potential EMP attacks.

Let's finally consider the fifth set of national security threats that are causing America's moral outrage before the critical presidential election of 2016.

The Threats Posed by Potential Major Cyber Hacks, Cyber Attacks, and Physical Sabotage on America's Critical Infrastructure. These potential threats are against: (1) military secrets, command, control, computers, communications, weapons systems, readiness, other technology, and personnel information; (2) power plants, electric grid, natural gas systems and facilities; (3) oil production, refining and distribution infrastructure; (4) water storage reservoirs, water quality and safety; (5) economic, financial, commercial, banking, and communications targets; (6) air traffic control systems, airports, commercial aircraft, other transportation infrastructure; and (7) consumer credit, financial, healthcare, and lifestyle information.

It's unfortunate, but true nevertheless. America is being hit by cyber hacks and cyber attacks repeatedly and probably at an ever increasing rate. America also appears to be experiencing physical sabotage to its infrastructure as well, although those behind such attacks are often difficult to determine. It is a challenge for authorities to determine in some cases if attacks are perpetrated by hostile nations, terrorists groups, sleeper terrorist cells, or isolated individuals, who suffer from mental disorders or who are disgruntled former employees.

Indeed, there are a number of distinct national security threats posed by hostile nations or terrorist groups that might seek to access and gain vital information, as well as compromise, shut down, damage or destroy our critical infrastructure. The threatened infrastructure includes all the areas listed above that span military, electric power, natural gas, oil and gasoline, water, finance, commercial activities, banking, communications, air traffic control, and consumer information.

Consider these ominous cyber threats. Hostile nations or terrorists might try accessing, damaging or entirely shutting down our electric grid, large power plants, big city water systems, critical infrastructure choke points, or other systems that support our lives. Similarly, suppose they target cell phone infrastructure facilities or other key communications systems to neutralize our communications capabilities. Banking and financial systems, things like ATM networks and check processing facilities, are also potential terrorist targets that can disrupt our lives. The air traffic control system is another prime target as well.

Let's look at just a few quick examples to gain a sense of the magnitude of the threats posed and the reasons why Americans are genuinely concerned about our national security.

Recall what happened in the fall of 2014 when an air traffic control facility was sabotaged near Chicago. It took days to restore the air traffic system and get all scheduled flights running again. According to the Chicago Tribune, thousands of flights were delayed and some passengers were stranded for up to two weeks. The Chicago Tribune also reported: "Airline losses were estimated at $350 million."[165]

Indeed, even one small cyber attack can cause untold financial losses and inconvenience to thousands of Americans as the Chicago area air traffic control facility illustrates. A major cyber attack can prove to be far more destructive and costlier in terms of a human death toll and in substantial financial losses in the billions of dollars. For example, one report cited in Forbes states that: "A major cyber attack on the U.S. electric grid could cause over a $1 trillion in economic impact and roughly $71.1 billion in insurance claims ..." The scenario in that report was a cyber attack on the northeastern electric grid causing a blackout in 15 States and the District of Columbia.[166]

According to one news source, there were almost 61,000 cyber attacks and security breaches against the Federal government in one year alone.[167] In the private sector, PricewaterhouseCoopers (PwC) reported that global cyber attacks were up 48% in 2014 to a total number of 48 million attacks.[168] That's a staggering statistic.

Let's look at one final sobering example of physical sabotage.

It took place at PG&E Corporation's Metcalf transmission substation in the San Jose, California area. It started with someone cutting AT&T fiber-optic telecommunications cables in a manner that made it particularly difficult to repair. This was followed by snipers targeting and knocking out 17 large transformers by selectively hitting their oil-filled cooling systems to permit the transformers to overheat before shutting down. The entire incident took only about one hour to pull off.

Some important points about this act of sabotage. During the attack more than 100 shell casings were left behind that are similar to AK-47 shell casings. Of note, the shell casings didn't have any fingerprints on them, a sign that the attack was well planned. Small rock piles were also found in the area that might have been left by an advance person, who wanted to point out best sites for targeting the transformers.[169] Finally, according to *The Wall Street Journal*:

> To some, the Metcalf incident has lifted the discussion of serious U.S. grid attacks beyond the theoretical. "The breadth and depth of the attack was unprecedented" in the

U.S., said Rich Lordan, senior technical executive for the Electric Power Research Institute. The motivation, he said, "appears to be preparation for an act of war."[170]

Americans should be deeply concerned with the threats posed by potential major cyber hacks, cyber attacks, and physical sabotage on America's critical infrastructure.

Besides the issues dealing with morality and freedom, the moral outrage of voters as we approach the critical presidential election of 2016 is being stoked by the national security issues we just discussed, along with a number of vital economic security issues. These issues are also on the minds of voters and are causing considerable moral outrage as well. Let's turn out attention to these issues of economic security right now.

What are the Economic Security Issues adding to the Moral Outrage of Americans?

As a result of years of foolish progressive socialist policies and programs, America's economy is anemic, weak and struggling. Americans in turn are the ones living through this awful economy.

The Wall Street Journal reported that our economy is in the "worst expansion" since World War II, a troubling economic fact. Indeed, since the end of the last recession in 2009, the American Economy has limped along at only an average rate of 2.2% growth annually, which is more than one half of one percent lower than the next worse recovery in the last 70 years.[171]

Bottom line, this is the worst economic recovery America has lived through in 70 years.[172] It's a pathetic result for progressive socialism and its ever-failing economic philosophy. For those who study progressive socialism from a pro-economic growth perspective, these results are anticipated and expected. Economic freedom results in economic growth. In stark contrast, socialism inhibits economic growth.

Lack of Jobs and Economic Growth. The most immediate impact on Americans when there is a lack of economic growth as measured by GDP growth is that it's far more difficult to get a new job, or change jobs; or if you are a new graduate from high school or college, it's far more challenging to get your first job. Lack of jobs is a tough reality Americans are dealing with today and a major cause of additional moral outrage over how the nation's economy is being thwarted by progressives. Let's look deeper at the lack of jobs America faces today.

Currently, there are over 94 million Americans of working age, who are not working, according to the Bureau of Labor Statistics. The "participation rate" is a dismal 62.6%.[173] The participation rate hasn't been this low since October 1977 when it hit 62.4% during the Carter administration. That was nearly four decades ago.[174]

Parenthetically, the participation rate is the percentage of the population that is currently working, or that is available and actively seeking work. When the participation rate is low, it can mean many people are either not working or are not actively seeking employment or both.[175]

Unfortunately, a civilian labor force participation rate of 62.6% means that 37.4% of Americans aren't participating in the civilian labor force, a sad fact for those unwillingly impacted and a bleak statistic for America's economy and economic growth.

Just think. Americans, who are forced to be idle due to a lack of job opportunities, are not able to contribute their education, knowledge, talents and skills to building a better life for themselves and their families, as well as to creating a more robust and prosperous economy for America. For these Americans, it's a "lose-lose" situation; they lose and the entire economy loses too.

While the current official unemployment rate from the government seems rosy at 5.1%, it masks the higher U-6 measure of unemployment that is now 10.3%. This measure includes those who have looked for jobs and given up as well as those who have accepted part time work when they couldn't find the full time work they sought. This metric in many ways is a more accurate gauge of unemployment. It shows us the extent to which workers are not being fully employed within the economy.[176]

For these many suffering Americans, big government continues to throttle back the economy with progressive socialist fiscal (taxation and spending), regulatory, and monetary policies that stifle economic growth and prosperity. Literally for many Americans, big government forces them into a life of financial frustration, and sometimes even, government dependency against their own free will. No wonder their moral outrage continues unabated and fuels the critical presidential election of 2016.

Disastrous Effects of ObamaCare. The second major economic security issue impacting Americans before the critical presidential election of 2016 is ObamaCare and its debilitating effects on the American healthcare system and on American family budgets.

ObamaCare has been an unmitigated progressive socialist failure. ObamaCare is expensive. It's bureaucratic. Moreover, ObamaCare is an obstacle to innovation and price reductions with the regulatory morass and complexity it creates, as well as the confusion it causes among both healthcare providers and patients alike.

Plus, ObamaCare's website has been a technical nightmare, debuting on October 1st, 2013 among some fanfare and collapsing soon thereafter.[177] It was also the object of some ridicule because of its astounding price tag. It's incredible to imagine; but, according to one study, the ObamaCare website enrollment system itself cost about $2.1 billion dollars.[178]

Instead of lowering healthcare premiums, ObamaCare has caused them to skyrocket. Assuming you're fortunate enough to keep your insurance plans (many Americans have lost the plans that they wanted to keep), co-payments and deductibles might be higher too. Plus, the outlook for further premium increases appears likely on the horizon.

To illustrate, the largest health plan in Tennessee, BlueCross BlueShield of Tennessee, raised their rates a significant 36.3% for 2016. In another example, Oregon's Moda Health Plan Inc. increased their average rate 25.6%. Moda Health Plan Inc. is the biggest health plan on Oregon's state exchange.[179] In one last example of the increasing costs of health insurance premiums, consider Florida. Regulators in the State of Florida indicate that health insurance premiums for those who purchase their own plans in Florida will rise 9.5% in 2016.[180]

While the actual numbers vary by State and health insurance company, the trend is quite clear. Health insurance premiums are going up significantly.

Adding to the data on the adverse impact of ObamaCare on health insurance premiums, a National Bureau of Economic Research study published by the Brookings Institution shows that non-group premiums have increased in 45 States.[181]

The National Bureau of Economic Research study helps to prove the point that government interference in a market leads to economic inefficiencies and higher costs. Such government intervention also tends to lead to less innovation, more shortages, as well as lower quality products and services in a given market.

As mentioned above, it's not just health insurance premiums that are going up. Deductibles are hurting American individuals and families. Take the case of employer-based healthcare plans. Around 150 million Americans are covered by employer-based plans. Often, deductibles are so high that people just skip the healthcare they really need.[182] All of this is largely caused by ObamaCare's turning the economics of healthcare into upheaval and disarray, turmoil and confusion.

Consider just a few facts mentioned in *USA Today*:

> A recent Commonwealth Fund survey found that four in 10 working-age adults skipped some kind of care because of the cost, and other surveys have found much the same. The portion of workers with annual deductibles — what consumers must pay before insurance kicks in — rose from 55% eight years ago to 80% today, according to research by the Kaiser Family Foundation. And a Mercer study showed that 2014 saw the largest one-year increase in enrollment in "high-deductible plans" — from 18% to 23% of all covered

employees.[183]

Meanwhile the size of the average deductible more than doubled in eight years, from $584 to $1,217 for individual coverage.[184]

Overall, healthcare costs have soared and are continuing to climb with no relief in sight. In addition, not only have some Americans lost their health insurance plans; but in some cases, they have lost their favorite doctors and hospitals as well.

Bottom line, ObamaCare has negatively and dramatically impacted America's healthcare system and has contributed to the moral outrage voters feel against the politicians sent to Washington to repeal ObamaCare, who have failed to take action against this legislation, legislation that the American people never wanted in 2010 when it was originally voted on, and legislation that the American people hope to rid themselves of soon.

Out-of-Control Government Spending and National Debt. A third vital economic security issue that fuels the moral outrage of American voters is the growing fiscal irresponsibility of the Federal government.

The electorate intuitively understands that reckless spending and the mounting national debt (currently running between $18 trillion and $19 trillion) must end at some point in time to avoid a collective national default, an effective national bankruptcy, or a world-shaking global financial crisis.

To voters, it's simple common sense that doesn't require a Ph.D. in economics. Yet, the political parties will not take action. Voters are therefore angry, frustrated and upset. Their moral outrage grows and they intend to be heard on Election Day.

Excessive Regulation of the American Economy. The fourth and final major economic security issue fueling the moral outrage of voters prior to the critical presidential election of 2016 is the excessive and burdensome regulation of the American Economy.

From an economics viewpoint, regulations are an enormous drain on productivity and awkwardly restrain the engines of economic freedom and free enterprise. Regulations tend to prevent new businesses from starting, and they tend to hold back existing businesses from growing and thriving. While ostensibly created for some good purpose in mind, they seem to fall into the category of useless nuisances. Let's look at an example.

Trey Garrison, in writing about the mortgage servicing industry, discusses how regulations are choking the mortgage service business. In his view, regulations are not only stifling mortgage service providers, but consumers as well. The "mortgage disclosure avalanche" is literally burying consumers. The regulations are simply too complicated and complex.[185] In Trey Garrison's words:

> These backwards rules are crafted where everything not forbidden is mandatory and everything not mandatory is forbidden. The laws are designed to protect the lowest common denominator, the kind of people who are the reason there are tags on hair dryers warning you not to use it while in the shower. No wonder the disclosure forms alone are as long as they are.[186]

With convoluted complexity comes another problem for those regulated, compliance. How does an industry comply with rules and regulations that are arcane and incomprehensible? Or, regulations that are constantly changing? It's downright frustrating and demoralizing. Of course, it's also a roadblock to productivity.

Let's think about another set of regulations that impact Americans significantly on an individual level and throttles our economy on a macro level scale. This set of regulations goes by the term "land use restrictions."[187]

Have you ever thought about how some areas of the country are hotbeds of innovation, industry, jobs and wealth (such as Silicon Valley located roughly between San Francisco and San Jose)? In contrast, have you realized that other geographical parts of the country languish economically? Of course, there are the expected reasons. Access to educational institutions and low cost energy might be two obvious factors that encourage and foster productivity and economic growth. But, possibly a less recognized factor is the availability of human capital.[188]

In America's past, labor moved from less productive areas of the country to more productive areas to find better jobs. This resulted in more prosperity and economic growth. However, today, land use restrictions hinder housing supply in some places, especially along the coastal areas of California. Without a sufficient supply of housing that people can pay for with their anticipated incomes, human capital is limited in its mobility and the economy is limited in its growth potential.[189]

Land use restrictions are just another regulatory burden on the American Economy. Certainly, with reduced controls on housing development, new businesses, new jobs, and new economic growth would spring up.

Let's move from these two examples to the larger picture. Excessive regulation has a considerable overall impact on the economy. According to the Competitive Enterprise Institute's annual study of Federal regulations:

> Federal regulation and intervention cost American consumers and businesses an estimated $1.88 trillion in 2014 in lost economic productivity and higher prices.
>
> If U.S. federal regulation was a country, it would be the world's 10th largest economy, ranking behind Russia and ahead of India.
>
> Economy-wide regulatory costs amount to an average of $14,976 per household – around 29 percent of an average family budget of $51,100. Although not paid directly by individuals, this "cost" of regulation exceeds the amount an average family spends on health care, food and transportation.[190]

It is worth pointing out that the above $1.88 trillion cost of regulations on the American people does not include State and local regulatory costs. It's strictly an estimate of the Federal regulatory burden on the American Economy.

No wonder Americans are angry, frustrated and upset at the government's intrusion into our lives and our pocketbooks. This economic security issue is one more reason that the electorate is morally outraged and that 2016 will be a critical presidential election year.

A Summary of the Reasons for the New Conservative Era

As we said early in the Chapter, America has a history of dealing with the need for change through ballots and peaceful political realignments. When American voters sense the moral principles articulated in the Declaration of Independence and the political principles encapsulated in the Constitution are being overlooked, or disregarded, or ignored, or flagrantly abused, Americans develop a sense of moral outrage. If, over a period of several elections, politicians, political parties and political institutions don't react and respond to the voter outrage adequately, citizens will take action at the voting booth.

Figure 2 summarizes the major reasons why Americans are morally outraged going into the presidential election of 2016. It is clear that America's moral outrage has reached a crescendo of disappointment, frustration and anger with the government because America's politicians, political parties and political institutions have failed to resolve these issues.

Prediction #2

On issue after issue, politicians have ignored the important problems that worry Americans. In election after election, political candidates have made promises to the American people and have gone into office and have not kept their promises. Political parties that stood for vital moral principles and political principles in the past have largely jettisoned their principles and left Americans to agonize over their future.

In the year 2016, Americans will speak loudly and clearly. They will

Figure 2 – Reasons for the New Conservative Era

Issues Dealing with Morality and Freedom
- Violating the Constitution and the Bill of Rights
- Violating the Separation of Powers
- Violating the Rule of Law
- Violating Domestic Peace – Rioting and Racial Tensions in Our Cities
- Violating Domestic Peace – A National Crime Wave

Issues Dealing with National Security
- The Threats Posed by America's Unprotected Borders and Illegal Immigration
- The Threats Posed by Potential Terrorist Attacks
- The Threats Posed by the Terrible Iran Nuclear Deal
- The Threats Posed by a Potential Electro-Magnetic Pulse (EMP) Attack on America and the Meltdown of America's Electric Grid
- The Threats Posed by Potential Major Cyber Hacks, Cyber Attacks, and Physical Sabotage on America's Critical Infrastructure

Issues Dealing with Economic Security
- Lack of Jobs and Economic Growth
- Disastrous Effects of ObamaCare
- Out-of-Control Government Spending and National Debt
- Excessive Regulation of the American Economy

be heard by the politicians, political parties and political institutions. The American voter will no longer be content with casual promises. They will look for strong evidence that political candidates have walked the walk and not merely paid lip service to America's ideals. Incumbents with a list of broken promises might want to dust off their old resumes.

The American voter will vote with their hearts, souls and minds.

Prediction #2. The presidential election of 2016 will be one of those relatively rare, critical presidential elections. It will be characterized by the largest voter turnout in absolute numbers and in percentage terms.

If there is any voter fraud during the election, it will be literally swamped by the historic turnout of active and energized conservative voters, newly re-energized conservative voters, as well as altogether new conservative voters. Many of these new conservative voters will be coming from the ranks of Americans, who are disillusioned with the grandiose promises and failed programs of progressive socialist politicians. Many too will be new Christian voters who are concerned with issues of morality and freedom, and especially with the perceived loss in religious liberty.

Surprising many pols and pundits and many established campaign consultants and media experts, there will be major political party realignments and political institution realignments.

This will be an exciting election to participate in and to watch.

Part II

The Critical Presidential Election of 2016 – The Battle for America's Bright Future

Chapter 3

The Critical Presidential Election of 2016

Get ready for one of the greatest political battles that has ever taken place in the world of electoral politics. It will pit the proponents of progressive socialism, socialism, Marxism, communism, and the welfare state against the American ideals of morality and freedom, liberty and limited government, free enterprise, free markets and free trade. It will be a monumental battle. It will be a culmination of the decades long culture war, the century long progressive war against our Constitution, and what I have termed in an earlier book *America's Economic War,* an ideological war between two diametrically opposed religious/cultural, political and economic systems, American capitalism and socialism.[191]

The critical presidential election of 2016 is the battle for America's future and whether or not it will be a bright future with morality and freedom, or a dismal future under oppressive, big government control and domination.

Why is this Presidential Election Truly the Battle for America's Bright Future?
Since the critical presidential election of 1896, progressive ideas have been at play in American politics. The goals of American progressivism was to redefine and repurpose the American principles found in the Declaration of Independence and in the Constitution. The moral principles in the Declaration of Independence and the political principles of the Constitution were the building blocks of American civilization. They were the concrete that formed the foundation of our truly exceptional nation. They defined our morality, protected our freedom, and guided our journey into the future.

Indeed, our moral and political principles empowered America to become the richest, most creative, most innovative, most productive, most economically successful, and the most generous nation ever to exist on the face of the earth.

But, heavily influenced by Karl Marx and other advocates of command and control thinking, an American version of "progressive" Marxism and socialism grew up on the North American continent. From the outset, it admired the European approach to government. This despite the fact that in the late 1700's, America had rejected the monarchy of King George and the European traditions associated with royalty. Article 1 Section 9 of the Constitution clearly admonished Americans against a culture led by royalty by stating: "No Title of Nobility shall be granted by the United States ..."

As outlined in Chapter 1 and explained within the discussion of American Constitutional Eras, progressives pushed forward their agenda for re-creating our Founding Fathers vision for the future of America. Woodrow Wilson attempted to morph our Constitutionally-protected freedom into his so-called "New Freedom." Other progressives persisted with faulty and unconstitutional Supreme Court decisions that read into the Constitution virtual legislation which no Congress had ever passed and no president had ever signed.

From the school board to the County Courthouse, from the State House to the House of Representatives and the Senate, from Congress to the Oval Office in the White House, progressive socialists have "progressed." In truth, they have "progressed" in carrying out a long term effort to re-shape America into a European style, socialist-Marxist country.

They sought a welfare state on a grand scale. The over $18 trillion and growing National Debt is evidence of the efforts that these progressive socialists have made. We must give them credit (and they really do like credit). It's an enormous task to borrow and spend enough to push the National Debt over $18 trillion dollars!

This phalanx of progressives is what stands between Americans and

America's bright future. Make no mistake about the seriousness of America's current Constitutional challenge. It's a moral crisis and a genuine threat to our freedom. It's also an economic crisis and a real threat to our prosperity.

If progressives continue to take America down the path of big government, enormous debt, fiscal irresponsibility, high risk monetary intervention, regulatory growth, highly limited freedom, and cultural disintegration, the price will be staggering.

We will lose morality both in and out of government. We will lose the Constitution and the Rule of Law. We will lose our freedoms across the board. We will fall into deep economic and social decline. We will be bankrupt morally and economically. We will likely be attacked militarily, unable to afford our own military defenses. We will come under the control of some totalitarian government or ideology. Or, we might face chaos and anarchy at the hands of evil, cruel and brutal terrorists, whose goal is to barbarically destroy our Western Civilization.

I believe in America and the American people. As Americans, we will not let America be destroyed. America faced grave crises in the past and the American people, as well as morality and freedom, always won out. It will happen again in 2016. It will play out in the critical presidential election of 2016. The American people will win in 2016. Morality and freedom will win again. America will have a bright future, even brighter than the past.

The phalanx of progressives is arrayed against America's basic moral and political principles. What will conservatives do to overcome this challenge?

How Will Conservatives Win the Battle for America's Bright Future?

Conservatives will decisively win the critical presidential election of 2016. It will also pick up conservative seats in the House and Senate. Conservatives will continue to take control of gubernatorial and legislative seats across America and will begin to control additional school boards from coast to coast.

As we will discuss later, there are common sense solutions to all the issues that have generated the current moral outrage felt by Americans. For example, the newly elected conservative president most likely will swiftly use Executive Orders to rescind previous bad and questionable Executive Orders. In addition, the new conservative president and Congress will quickly address national security issues and the important issues dealing with the lack of jobs and economic growth, as well as the repeal of ObamaCare.

In addition, as vacancies in the Supreme Court take place, the new president will fill the slots with conservatives that believe in an originalist interpretation of the Constitution and that believe in the Rule of Law. The new Supreme Court justices will not seek the guidance of law from other countries. The Supreme Court justices (as well as judges from other courts around America) will content themselves in interpreting the law, and no longer be legislating from the bench. Quite a few bad Supreme Court decisions from the past will probably be overruled as new appropriate cases reach the high court during the new Conservative Era.

How Will Conservatives Win the Critical Presidential Election of 2016?

Conservatives will win by taking the progressive threat very seriously. Conservatives will win by starting at the grassroots level. Conservatives will win by getting active themselves. Conservatives will win by talking to their families and relatives. Conservatives will win by speaking to their neighbors. Conservatives will win by establishing an overwhelming presence in social media – Facebook, Twitter, LinkedIn, Instagram, Pinterest, Google+, YouTube, and other websites that will empower them to reach out and engage others.

Voters will mobilize themselves out of an overwhelming sense of purpose and urgency, not seen often in American History.

Conservatives will win because active and energized voters will be involved in the election. Conservatives will win because newly re-energized voters will be involved in the election again. Conservatives will win because altogether new voters will become involved in the election for the first time. As mentioned at the end of the last Chapter, many of these new conservative voters will be coming from the ranks of Americans, who are disillusioned with the grandiose promises and failed programs of progressive socialist politicians.

Conservatives will win because groups of voters will fragment their monolithic support and break away from their former loyalties based on identity politics. These groups will splinter their support and will shift their party affiliations and allegiances. Indeed, these voters will be involved in the election in new ways, and in supporting new candidates, and in aligning with different principles. Plus, some conservatives will choose to run for office for the first time, out of a sense of patriotism and duty to country.

Old interest groups will shatter in 2016 as political parties and political institutions are substantially realigned, restructured, reformed and remade.

Conservatives will win because voter turnout in absolute terms and percentage terms will be the largest in the history of American presidential elections. This large voter turnout will be fueled in part by a 21st century "campaign of education"[192] similar to that used in the critical presidential election of 1896 discussed earlier.

In this case, the 21st century "campaign of education" will likely encourage new support for conservative principles and common sense solutions to the challenges confronting America. Most importantly, it will help to bring in tens of millions of new voters into the election. Of course, this large voter turnout is certainly a sign of a historic election and a critical presidential election.

The Battle for America's Bright Future and the critical presidential election of 2016 is so vitally important to America and to Americans that active conservatives, re-energized conservatives, and brand new conservatives will join in the fray and change America's electoral landscape for more than a generation to come.

The Battle for America's Bight Future and the critical presidential election of 2016 will be won by conservatives who are morally outraged by issues of morality and freedom, national security, and economic security. All of the issues we discussed in some detail in the previous Chapter will motivate and energize conservatives.

The results of this victory are straight forward. The current sense of grave crisis will recede into American History. The Anti-Constitutional Era will end quickly and precipitously. The Conservative Era will commence rapidly and dramatically. America will return to building a bright future of peace and prosperity once again, in its long and exceptional history.

Prediction #3

The Battle for America's Future will be won decisively in an extraordinary, conservative landslide victory in the critical presidential election of 2016. The popular vote and the Presidential Electoral College vote will be won by the conservative candidate in an overwhelming landslide victory, similar in size to Ronald Reagan's two electoral landslides in 1980 and 1984.

Chapter 4

The Third Conservative Election Landslide within a Decade

With the rush of events over the last few years and the incredible list of issues the nation faces, it's understandable if conservatives overlook some of their victories. Just consider the election in 2010. Thanks to conservative voters, the House of Representatives was captured in a historic conservative landslide. But, you say, the House of Representatives does not always act conservatively. True enough. But, without conservative voters, the House would still be in the control of a different party.

In a similar fashion, the 2014 election was another historic election. In the election of 2014, the Senate was captured in a second conservative landslide. Once again, conservative voters are frustrated by the lack of decisive conservative action on the part of many Senators that were sent to Washington to solve issues that concern Americans.

Let's take a few moments to examine the conservative landslides of 2010 and 2014 and reflect on the progress conservatives have made. Then, let's project forward to 2016 when conservatives capture the White House in the third conservative election landslide within a decade.

The First Conservative Election Landslide within a Decade – Capturing the House in 2010

It was a stunning rout for progressives in the Congressional elections of 2010. In a historic landslide for conservative voters, the Republican Party picked up 63 seats in the House of Representatives, garnering a remarkable 242 total seats versus 193 seats for the Democratic Party.[193] In the Senate, while not gaining control, conservatives pushed Republican candidates into winning an additional six seats, inching ever closer to control of the Senate. This left Democratic Senators with a smaller 53 to 47 seat control of the U. S. Senate.[194]

On the gubernatorial front, conservatives catapulted Republicans to a 29 to 20 majority of governorships with one independent governor bringing the total to 50 States.[195]

Adding to these numbers, in State legislative elections across America, conservatives propelled Republicans to win 675 additional seats and to make legislative bodies from 15 States change hands from Democratic Party control to Republican Party control. In some of these 15 States both the House and Senate chambers switched party control. In one State, both the Assembly and Senate switched control to the Republican Party.[186] Naturally, these are rather dramatic results, signaling a powerful political undercurrent and a strong momentum that was building during 2010. Its strength also portended an emerging, future trend.

What caused conservatives to capture the House in 2010 in a commanding landslide and widely capture governorships and State legislatures across the American political landscape? One factor was the change in heart that some religious Americans brought to the election. Three groups, Protestant/Other Christian, Catholic, and Unaffiliated all increased their support for House Republican candidates. However, Catholics not only increased their support, they also switched their overall favor to the Republican Party. In the prior two Congressional elections, Catholics favored Democratic Party candidates by double-digit margins. That's a significant change favoring overall conservative momentum.[197]

What were the big issues going into the 2010 elections? The American Economy and its lackluster recovery after the recession, the lack of jobs, and the tremendous deficit were probably the top issues in the 2010 elections. Close behind was ObamaCare, the system passed over the will of the American people, that tinkered with a healthcare system most Americans considered good. The imaginary healthcare crisis touted by progressives simply didn't exist in the minds of a large majority of Americans in poll after poll. Recall that ObamaCare passed Congress and was signed by the president in March of 2010. Another important issue was illegal immigration, a problem that was still not resolved to the satisfaction of the American people.

Déjà vu - All Over Again? Do all those critical issues from 2010 sound familiar to you? They are certainly very similar to the issues generating moral outrage in the electorate as we enter the critical presidential election of 2016.

Conservatives helped the Republican Party regain control of the House in 2010 precisely to resolve these issues. Fix the economy, increase the number and quality of jobs, cut the deficit, rein in spending, repeal or defund ObamaCare, fix the broken border, and stop illegal immigration. Obviously, those issues continue to fester and to go unresolved.

Unfortunately, the House victory did not get the desired results voters sought. Voters were angry, frustrated and upset. It was said by the politicians, the House is not enough. We need to control the Senate as well. Of course, the 2012 presidential election came next.

In 2012, conservatives were disturbed and discouraged when a conservative was not selected to be the Republican presidential nominee. Conservatives treaded water for two more years. The stage was set for the 2014 election.

The Second Conservative Election Landslide within a Decade – Capturing the Senate in 2014

Since capturing the House in a landslide election in 2010 did not resolve the issues facing America, conservatives stepped up to the plate again in 2014 and in another historic landslide election, captured the Senate shocking many pols, pundits, political insiders and political consultants.

Conservatives helped the Republican Party take over control of the Senate by picking up eight additional Senate seats. That meant

Republicans had a 54 to 46 vote margin in the Senate, a remarkable change in the makeup of the upper chamber. Among the seven seats designated as tossup races, Republicans won Senate seats in Alaska, Colorado, Georgia, Iowa, Kansas, and North Carolina. The Democratic Party picked up the final tossup State, New Hampshire.[198]

Conservatives also aided Republicans in increasing the number of seats it held in the House by 13, bringing the Republican Party control to 247 to 188.[199] This positive result was the best House Republicans had done since 1947 – 1949, during President Truman's tenure of office.[200] That's nearly 70 years earlier. Of course, this also meant Congress was now firmly in the hands of the Republican Party, thanks in large measure to conservatives, who were still angry, frustrated and upset with the daunting issues facing America, and who made sure they got out and voted.

On the legislative front, further inroads were made by conservatives. After the 2014 elections, the GOP gained control of an astounding 70% of all State legislative chambers. It also resulted in 24 States being completely controlled by Republicans – that means that the GOP held the governor's mansion and controlled both State legislative chambers in 24 different States.[201]

What were the big issues going into the 2014 elections? The answer to this question seems clear. Once again, the economy was at the top of the list for conservatives. It included such related issues as the lack of availability of good jobs, the persistent Federal deficit question, and high taxes. In addition, voters were quite concerned over Islamic militants in Iraq and Syria and illegal immigration.[202]

Déjà vu – Again? Do these issues sound familiar again? The issues match closely with the issues preceding the 2010 landslide election. The electorate continued to tell the politicians and political parties in 2014 what they truly wanted.

Indeed, the 2014 election cycle saw the second conservative landslide election within a decade with sweeping victories across America, including capturing the Senate.

The Third Conservative Election Landslide within a Decade – Capturing The White House in 2016

Having captured the House in 2010 and the Senate in 2014, the conservative momentum driving America into the new Conservative Era continues unabated. In 2016, the goal is the biggest yet. The third conservative election landslide will deal the progressives a political knockout punch by capturing The White House.

What Can We Expect Politically from this Third Conservative Election Landslide? After the critical presidential election of 2016, conservatives will control two branches of government – the Executive branch and the legislative branch. Both the House and the Senate will be under decisive conservative control. Conservatives will also be in a likely position to remake the Supreme Court with probably four new appointments to the Supreme Court by the president in the few years following 2016.

Progressive Supreme Court justices that winked at the Constitution to promote a progressive socialist agenda and to actively legislate from the bench will be replaced with solid conservative justices with a strong affinity for an original interpretation of the Constitution, guaranteeing our fundamental liberties, and upholding the Rule of Law.

Lower courts will follow the lead of the Supreme Court in the new Conservative Era, as attrition on the bench gives way to the appointment of new conservative judges across America. It's possible that Congress under Article 3 will choose to gut certain courts deemed to have gone over the edge in judicial activism and will choose to create new courts that are thought helpful to restore the rightful power of the American people and the Rule of Law. Just the fact that Congress has Article 3 power to oversee the lower courts will help to rein in seemingly out-of-control judicial activism.

In addition, prior gains in the House and Senate will be solidified with additional new seats taken in the House and Senate.

Importantly, and in one sense under the radar of many observers, will be some subtle changes. In the election of 2016, some moderate Republicans will decide to retire from Congress before their next election, others will decide not to run for reelection, and still others will not win their primary battles. But, in nearly all cases, these moderates will be replaced by conservatives. That means, the post-election numbers, will not completely reflect the extent, the breadth and the depth of "how conservative America will truly be" at the beginning of the new Conservative Era.

The critical presidential election of 2016 will result in the third conservative election landslide within a decade and will result in conservatives capturing The White House. What else can we say about the critical presidential election of 2016? There are actually a number of points that can be made.

What Will Distinguish this Third Conservative Election Landslide from Other Presidential Elections? To start with, of course, it will be a landslide victory for conservatives. It will be both a popular vote landslide for the winning presidential candidate as well as a Presidential Electoral College landslide.

In addition, in the presidential race, a "comprehensive conservative" who supports conservative principles across the board, versus a "cafeteria conservative" that picks and chooses what subset of conservative principles they choose to support and defend, will be elected president. More about "comprehensive conservatives" and "cafeteria conservatives" comes later in this book.

Also, more about what party the winning conservative presidential candidate will likely represent will come a little later in this book as well. The ideas of a potential third party or an emerging new party are not out of the realm of possible scenarios we might encounter in the critical presidential election of 2016. These possibilities are discussed in a subsequent Chapter in some detail.

This election will also mean conservatives win in many other State and local elections throughout America ranging from gubernatorial mansions, to State legislative chambers, to county courthouses, to school boards. The impact will be far-ranging.

Recall that a new political communications media is often associated with a critical presidential election. Just as the pamphlet, the newspaper, the mass circulation press, and television impacted earlier critical presidential elections, the changing role of the media will characterize this election.

We will see the end of the mainstream media as we have known it over the last few decades. Its influence on shaping American voting patterns will be greatly diminished as I have previously written and discussed on Talk Radio programs. In its place, we will witness the rise of the new media that includes the ever popular and growing conservative Talk Radio programs and various other social media websites and apps.

Along with the landslide victory for conservatives, will come high voter turnout. This, of course, is another significant characteristic of a critical presidential election. Expect a record high voter turnout in 2016.

Political party realignments associated with the critical presidential election of 2016 will necessitate new political party leaders and new political leaders at the national, State and local levels. Nearly all political leaders in power will be replaced by early 2017. It will seem like a new day in Washington after the critical presidential election of 2016. It will also seem like a new day across America.

Prediction #4

One of the primary reasons for all three of the conservative election landslides within the short space of a decade is the moral outrage of American voters that we have discussed earlier in this book. Americans are angry, frustrated and upset with their politicians who have not developed the solutions they sought to the issues that concern Americans.

Prediction #4. One major result of the moral outrage of voters will be a dramatic realignment of the Republican Party and the Democratic Party. There is also a chance a new third party will arise and replace one of the current major two parties.

Part III

Impact on Major Political Parties

Chapter 5

A New Republican Party?

Conservatives are angry, frustrated and upset with the Republican Party. Other voters that sometimes vote for Republican candidates are also angry, frustrated and upset, albeit for slightly different reasons.

Consider this one telling result from a Fox News poll in 2015: "... 62 percent of Republican primary voters feel "betrayed" by politicians in their party." Quite a startling statement, except if you realize at the time of the poll, voters were fast approaching the critical presidential election of 2016.[203]

The Republican Party and many of its politicians have repeatedly disappointed their constituents. Often, conservatives are appalled at the lack of life and the lack of fight in their elected representatives. Certainly, their inability "to get the job done" is of paramount concern.

To conservatives and other voters, Republican candidates have expressed their apparent political philosophy during campaigns, have conveyed their beliefs, have articulated forthrightly they were conservatives, and have made promise after promise that they would go back to Washington and resolve the issues facing America. Yet, once in office, once back in Washington, their spines have weakened like jellyfish, their lives have become listless and enervated, their energy has dissipated and evaporated, and their ability and capability to represent their constituents has completely vanished into thin air.

American voters will not tolerate for long those elected officials, who don't perform according to their wishes. Similarly, American voters will not tolerate for long political parties that don't live up to their expectations. At a minimum, a few presidential election cycles is all that it takes for the electorate to become completely alienated from a major party. Without question, neither politicians nor political parties can take the American voter for granted, although they certainly try to do so in many cases.

In response to the moral outrage of voters, political parties will change somehow or they will cease to exist in the long run. Political parties will evolve, will reinvent themselves, will morph, will changes their names, will change their political positions, will change their political platforms, will change their philosophies, will change their leaders, or will take some combination of these actions in order to deal with the moral outrage of voters when that moral outrage is building to a crescendo.

Otherwise, American voters will take their votes on a political shopping trip and will find another political party … or will start another political party … and the current alienated political party will simply go out of business. They will cease to exist and they will be relegated to the back pages of American History.

America has always had a free market in political parties. If you don't believe that, just remember the Whig Party or any of the parties that no longer exist in American politics.

Will We See the Republican Party (as we know it) End in 2016?

Most certainly, the Republican Party as we have known it for decades will end abruptly with the critical presidential election of 2016. The moral outrage of conservatives and others is palpable. The Republican Party (as we know it) has served its purpose in American History. It's now time to move into the next American Constitutional Era, the new Conservative Era, with a party that represents the views of Americans who strongly believe in morality and freedom. It will also be a party that will work hard and fight hard with the opposition, if needed, to solve the pressing problems and issues we as a nation face today.

Americans want a party that will return to the moral principles of the Declaration of Independence and the political principles of the Constitution. In other times of apparent crisis throughout

American History, voters rebooted the political parties to correspond to our traditional values of morality and freedom. The critical presidential election of 2016 is no different. Voters will not leave the Republican Party the same as we have known it for decades. The critical presidential election of 2016 will be the engine of change.

Will We See a New "Republican" Party in 2016?

One possibility for the current "Republican" Party is to morph into a new "Republican" Party that espouses viewpoints congruent with the values and opinions and solutions Americans seek now. You might call this the "Revitalized Republican" Party. This can happen by the Republican primary and caucus voters selecting a comprehensive conservative candidate that shares their views. Of course, the Republican National Convention would then ratify that selection for the nomination to be formally approved.

In this case, the party name can officially stay the same, but the philosophy and party leaders will change. You might call this a new Republican Party. However, it would still be the Republican Party, although revitalized and changed in many significant ways.

In my view, the moral outrage is so great and the Republican Party brand so damaged within the minds of the members of the Republican Party that its name will disappear from American politics. In its place, a newly named party will take its place. For operating convenience and efficiency, the party structure and functions will remain the same, but it will operate under a new name.

Just think of the Republican Party as a corporation. Its name will change, but its structures and functions will survive the name change. Recognize that leadership, management and even constituencies will dramatically change in the process. This is similar to a corporation getting a new CEO and bringing in a new management team and seeking to encourage new customers to buy its products and services.

Will We See a New Conservative Party in 2016?

Indeed, because the Republican Party name has been so tarnished and because the Republican Party has effectively abandoned many of its core principles, the Republican Party will rename itself to reflect its recommitment to traditional American beliefs and values. One potential new name for the Republican Party is the Conservative Party. Of course, political strategists and party members can invent many other appropriate names.

Prediction #5

The Republican Party (as we know it) will cease to exist as the "Republican Party" with the critical presidential election of 2016. The Republican Party under the leadership of a strong and solid, comprehensive conservative presidential nominee (and later, under the leadership of the new conservative president) will move to rename itself as the "Conservative Party."

The Conservative Party will be a stable party committed to the Declaration of Independence and the Constitution, the Rule of Law, morality and freedom, peace through a strong military defense, and prosperity through strong economic growth.

The Conservative Party will lead America into the new Conservative Era and America's Bright Future that will result from its core conservative principles.

Chapter 6

A New Democratic Party?

Traditional Democratic Party voters are upset with their party too. Interestingly, they are angry, frustrated and upset for completely different reasons than their conservative counterparts. Let's look at their rationale for anger against the Democratic Party in general, and Democratic Party politicians, in particular.

The Uber Left. First, many progressives, progressive socialists, socialists, Marxists, communists and anarchists – the "uber left" – feel the Democratic Party is too weak and too slow in its progression toward socialism and Marxism. Some probably even would prefer outright communism as the ideal form of government for America. Of course, the uber left disdains the morality and freedom of our Founding Fathers.

Instead, their values gravitate more toward a welfare state, pure socialism, or atheistic communism. They are often statist and totalitarian. For them, morality and freedom are mere roadblocks on the road to power for the uber elite and on the road to serfdom for everyone else. For them, too, the Democratic Party is just too slow dragging this reluctant country into socialism.

Minorities that Vote as a Monolithic Bloc. A second group of voters, who are getting more and more discontent with the Democratic Party, will be shocking to many pols, pundits, political insiders and political consultants. This second group consists of the minority voters who have consistently and monolithically supported Democratic Party candidates.

Many of these minority voters (and potential voters) and their families, relatives and friends have supported the Democratic Party for years, if not their entire lives. Some have supported the Democratic Party for generations. Many bought into the Democratic Party line that Republicans were evil, or at the very least, didn't care about minorities. Many bought into the Democratic Party's constant recitation of their good intentions to "fix" the system with more government programs, more money, and bigger government in general.

Many of these minority voters live in the inner cities; many are economically disadvantaged; many are suffering from crime in their neighborhoods and close to home; many are lingering in chronic unemployment and can't find good jobs (or even mediocre jobs); and many are simply emotionally drained and physically tired of being angry at the system, and trapped in circumstances they don't control.

But, more importantly, many of these minorities going into the critical presidential election of 2016 believe that the Democratic Party has not lived up to its promises, does not have its best interests in mind, has not solved its problems, and has not brought them peace and prosperity. Recently, many in the minority community realize that the Democratic Party no longer upholds its true family values.

Politically, many minority voters feel like the Democratic Party has taken them for granted for too long. They are disillusioned with the Democratic Party and are ready to forego their support and bolt the party.

JFK Democrats. The third group of Democratic Party Voters who are upset with their party and its values on the issues are what I call JFK Democrats. These Democratic Party voters are similar in values to John F. Kennedy and Scoop Jackson in certain ways and to Martin Luther King, Jr. and Joe Lieberman in other ways. These supporters in part helped give Ronald Reagan two landslide victories in 1980 and 1984. At that time, many of these supporters were referred to as "Reagan Democrats."

Their discontent and dissatisfaction with the Democratic Party stems from the fact that they believe the Democratic Party has abandoned them and their traditional American values for more uber left politics.

Will We See the Democratic Party (as we know it) End in 2016?

Yes, it is highly likely that before, during or after the critical presidential election of 2016 season, the Democratic Party (as we know it) will end in 2016. The current fracturing of the Democratic Party will continue unabated, until it is completely redefined or until it ceases to exist.

Will We See a New "Democratic" Party in 2016?

No, as with the Republican Party, the Democratic Party has evolved over recent decades. The Democratic Party has come to embrace the philosophy and policies of the uber left. A "Revitalized" Democratic Party will probably not take place.

I don't expect the Democratic Party to redefine its outreach to the minority community adequately and effectively. It will most probably continue to take minority groups for granted. It's also probably not going back to the days or the policies of JFK.

Will We See a New Progressive Socialist Party in 2016?

In keeping with its uber left philosophy and policies, which are clearly at odds with the Founding Fathers, the Declaration of Independence, and the Constitution, I think a strong case can be made for the Democratic Party to re-label itself as the "Progressive Socialist Party." It certainly is more accurate and intellectually honest. I also think its uber left supporters will feel more at home.

Their uber left supporters will now have their vision and objectives for America out in the open for all to see. They will no longer have to hide their true intentions. They will no longer have to hide what "hope and change" they seek for America and what "transformation" that they had in mind. Their agenda will be available for all to see and for all to consider, and for nearly all to reject emphatically and categorically.

Prediction #6

The Democratic Party (as we know it) will end in 2016. It will be a victim of the moral outrage of American voters. In the effort to steer its ship forward (from their vantage point), leading Democratic Party politicians will change the name of the party. The "Progressive Socialist Party" will take the place of the Democratic Party.

As a result of its uber-left philosophy and policies, it will be relegated to consistent second major party status in American politics during the forthcoming Conservative Era.

Chapter 7

A New Third Party?

Many people fear the rise of a third party because of the inherent confusion and chaos it might cause during this crucial time of grave crisis in America with serious issues on the minds of voters. I don't believe their fears are truly justified or that they need to worry at all. Let's think for a moment about the possibility of a third party candidate and the potential for a new third party.

Will We See a Third Party Candidate in 2016?

Realistically, there are at most only about two or three potential third party candidates in the wings that can sustain a run in the critical presidential election of 2016. If the newly named Conservative Party nominates a comprehensive conservative candidate, it is unlikely that a major third party candidate would attempt to pursue the presidency. The main reason for this conclusion is that such a third party candidate would have a formidable challenge too great to overcome, since the electorate appears ready to select a comprehensive conservative as president.

For a third party candidate to emerge, the Republican Party would need to remain as it is prior to the critical presidential election of 2016 and the Republican Party would further need to nominate a non-comprehensive conservative candidate instead. With a more "moderate" Republican in place, conservatives might walk away from the Republican Party and its nominee, and then, might place a comprehensive conservative into nomination from a new third party.

Given adequate financial resources, it's also credible to think someone might opt to nominate himself or herself to a newly created third party and run independently of the other two parties. Of course, the large price tag of pursuing such a strategy and the requirement of either self-funding this approach or raising sufficient campaign dollars for the run, make it doubtful anyone would try to do it, especially if a comprehensive conservative candidate is running on the Conservative Party ticket.

Will We See a Third Party Candidate Win in 2016?

There is only one scenario in which a third party candidate might be elected president. The parameters for that scenario include: (1) the Republican Party stays intact as it existed before 2016, (2) the Republican Party nominates a "moderate" Republican candidate that is unacceptable to conservative voters, (3) a comprehensive conservative candidate forms a new third party, and (4) the comprehensive conservative third party has the funding to launch and conduct a national campaign focused on the solutions conservative voters seek.

Teddy Roosevelt and the Bull Moose Party. Incidentally, it's interesting to note that when Teddy Roosevelt faced tough opposition by the Republican Party for their party's presidential nomination in June 1912, there was still enough time for him to form a viable third party. In this case, it was the well-known Bull Moose Party. Of course, his run for the presidency on the Bull Moose Party failed to get him elected president for a second time. He had previously won in 1904 as a Republican.[204]

I mention Teddy Roosevelt because some people think that a third party candidate has to start early to put together a reasonably good presidential campaign. Teddy Roosevelt was able to develop, launch and effectively run his presidential campaign in a matter of months between the Republican National Convention in June 1912 and the actual election.

Teddy Roosevelt's third party presidential campaign has a special distinction in American History. It was the only time in the 20th century that a third party presidential candidate received more popular votes and more electoral votes than one of the other two major party candidates. In the election of 1912, Woodrow Wilson (Democratic Party candidate) beat Theodore Roosevelt (Progressive or Bull Moose Party candidate), who in turn beat William Howard Taft (Republican Party candidate). Their respective popular vote percentages were: 42, 29 and 25. Their electoral counts respectively were: 435, 88 and 8.

Will We See a Third Party become a New Major Party in 2016?

If the above scenario falls into place and is successful, the comprehensive conservative third party candidate will become president and his or her newly formed party by default will become a de facto major party because its head is the President of the United States of America. In this instance, the moderate Republican Party candidate will lose the election and the Republican Party would fade into obscurity as well.

Prediction #7

There will be no major third party candidate in contention in the critical presidential election of 2016. Also, there will be no major new third party formed during 2016.

Part IV

Common Sense Solutions to the Issues Facing America

Chapter 8

The Core Principles

Americans by their nature are optimistic. Optimism is in our DNA. It stems in large measure from our founding, breaking away from a despotic monarch, asserting our freedom, proclaiming our God given "unalienable Rights, that among these are Life, Liberty, and the Pursuit of Happiness." These were in 1776, and continue to be today, profound thoughts and bold statements. They empower and energize America and Americans with enthusiasm, optimism, and a deep and abiding sense of hope.

An Optimistic Vision for America

In truth, America has an optimistic vision for itself and its future, for its individuals, for its families, for itself as a sovereign nation, and for a better tomorrow for all of us. This is the foundation for America's confidence and assurance, for America's innovation and creativity, and for America's spiritual and material growth.

It's also part of the fruit of an utterly unique American Exceptionalism that regrettably few in the narrow corridors of progressive socialist thought seem able to comprehend.

When American government, when American political institutions, when American political parties, when American politicians, stray from America's optimistic vision, change is inevitable.

Indeed, when the government distances itself from the people, by failing to adhere to the moral principles articulated in the Declaration of Independence, or by ceasing to respect the liberties guaranteed to the people by the Constitution, moral outrage develops over a period of time.

This moral outrage inevitably leads to a moral passion that refocuses the government on its guiding principles.

What are the Core Principles of the New Conservative Era?

Figure 3 conveniently sums up the core principles of the new Conservative Era. These principles will guide American leaders and American government throughout the Conservative Era. They are helpful to guide citizens as well.

The core principles of the new Conservative Era are divided into three key areas: (1) Morality and Freedom; (2) Peace through a Strong Military Defense; and (3) Prosperity through Strong Economic Growth. Morality and Freedom, Peace and Prosperity, are really the essence of what a morality-based government and a morality-based democracy should seek to preserve, protect and defend for its citizens.[205]

The three key areas and the 12 core principles are all essential for a nation to thrive. Missing any key area or any of the 12 core principles will diminish and weaken the important features of a nation that is founded on the unalienable Rights to Life, Liberty, and the Pursuit of Happiness.

For example, how long can a nation function and survive without morality in its government? Corruption destroys the fabric of a government and the entire nation. The elements of crony capitalism we have witnessed in recent years are mind-dumbing and add to the moral outrage citizens feel approaching the critical presidential election of 2016.

Similarly, in a world filled with terrorist groups that hate America and its freedom, and rogue nations that seek power over others and plunder for their own treasuries, without a strong national defense, how long can America protect its people and its sovereignty? A strong national defense is simple common sense. Its foolhardy to continue to eviscerate our military, reduce its numbers and strength, and expect it to maintain our freedom.

In the area of prosperity, America needs to follow proven pro-growth economic policies to move America forward. There is no need to have a lingering, job-less and anemic, economic recovery (if

Figure 3 – Core Principles of the New Conservative Era

Morality and Freedom
- We are committed to Morality throughout our government
- We are committed to Freedom for all individuals
- We are committed to upholding the Constitution
- We are committed to upholding the Rule of Law

Peace through a Strong Military Defense
- We are committed to maintaining a Strong Military Defense
- We are committed to maintaining a Secure Peace with all Nations
- We are committed to maintaining Secure Borders
- We are committed to maintaining our National Sovereignty

Prosperity through Strong Economic Growth
- We are committed to Pro-Growth Tax Policies
- We are committed to Pro-Growth Spending Policies
- We are committed to Pro-Growth Regulatory Policies
- We are committed to Pro-Growth Monetary Policies

it even rises to the level we can term "recovery").

America needs pro-growth tax policies, pro-growth spending policies, pro-growth regulatory policies, and pro-growth monetary policies. There is not enough space in this book to describe these policies, but the interested reader can read *Renewing America and Its Heritage of Freedom* for more information on economic freedom and pro-growth economic policies.[206]

The 12 core principles in Figure 3 form a framework for addressing all the issues that have spawned the moral outrage preceding the critical presidential election of 2016. I believe that these core principles will form the basis for the Conservative Era. I also believe that presidential candidates will be judged by the electorate on whether or not they will implement these principles if elected president. This brings up an interesting point. How do voters know whether a candidate for president, or for any other office for that matter, is a real conservative and is not just spouting words?

"Cafeteria Conservatives" versus "Comprehensive Conservatives"

At this time in American History, the word "conservative" is a plus in a general election. In the critical presidential election of 2016, it's even a more powerful word to encourage voters to support a candidate. In the past, we've all typically heard candidates talk of conservative positions they held and we gathered from their speeches that they were truly "conservative" in their philosophy and political inclinations.

Yet, many times, these same candidates return to Washington, only to frustrate voters when they suddenly lose their conservative values. It always seems amazing. Candidates get on a jet in their home States as conservatives. When they hit the tarmac at Dulles International Airport or Reagan National Airport, they become politicians with progressive views. Their minds and views appear to change dramatically. Do you think that these planes need more oxygen in their passenger cabins?

One way to differentiate "conservative" presidential candidates from one another (or for that matter, one way to differentiate Senate candidates or House candidates from one another), is to look at whether they are "cafeteria conservatives" or "comprehensive conservatives."

A "cafeteria conservative" believes in and adheres to some of the 12 core principles in Figure 3. For example, they might believe in peace through a strong national defense, but they don't adhere to strong pro-growth economic policies, preferring instead to advocate for various failed progressive socialist economic policies and programs.

Consider another illustration. Some fiscal policy "conservatives" that favor tax and spending pro-growth economic policies, might not favor strong support for the First and Second Amendments. Hence, they fall short in the area of commitment to upholding the Constitution. These are just a few possible examples. Many more actual examples might be encountered in races across America.

In contrast to "cafeteria conservatives," I recognize "comprehensive conservatives" as those conservatives who believe in, who defend, and who adhere to all 12 core principles of the new Conservative Era.

In my view, American voters are seeking a comprehensive conservative in the critical presidential election of 2016. I believe American voters want to resolve their moral outrage dealing with issues of morality and freedom, national security, and economic security. They hope to resolve all the issues we discussed earlier, all the issues that are propelling America into a new Conservative Era.

Prediction #8
The core principles presented in Figure 3 will guide America through the critical presidential election of 2016 – whether voters formally articulate them directly, or whether they informally act on them indirectly by voting for the presidential candidate that they believe will best resolve their moral outrage and solve the pressing issues facing America.

Americans will deal with their moral outrage over the American government, political parties, and political institutions that have failed to address voters' moral outrage and that have failed to solve America's vital issues related to morality and freedom, national security and economic security.

I predict America will elect a comprehensive conservative in the critical presidential election of 2016. I also predict the newly elected, comprehensive conservative president will follow the core principles of the new Conservative Era.

Chapter 9

Common Sense Solutions to the Issues of Morality and Freedom

Sitting at the top of concerns of the American voter are those issues dealing with morality and freedom. These are truly the foundational issues for the critical presidential election of 2016. Americans are worried that America, its morality including the morality of the government itself and the morality of elected officials, as well as its freedom are in danger of being extinguished by a relatively small group of progressives, socialists, Marxists, communists and anarchists who have somehow managed to take control of our government and hijacked our culture.

We have looked at these issues in some detail earlier in this book. Now, let's shift our attention and review solutions to the issues of morality and freedom in this Chapter. Plus, let's consider solutions to the other issues of national security and economic security in the subsequent two Chapters.

Recall that the first big concern with American voters is violating the Constitution and the Bill of Rights. What solutions do our core principles offer Americans in this time of grave concern and potential crisis?

Violating the Constitution and the Bill of Rights

Starting from the top and working down, the newly elected, comprehensive conservative president, the vice president, cabinet officers, agency directors and other officials of the new administration must preserve, protect and defend the Constitution of the United States of America. Let there be no hesitation or equivocation. All elected officials of the president's new administration and the entire Federal government complex must follow the Constitution.

In those instances where the Constitution has not been followed in recent years, new Executive Orders from the president and comparable administrative orders promulgated throughout departments and agencies must likewise follow the Constitution without question. The newly elected president can, for example, rescind Executive Orders from the previous president that appear to violate the Constitution or other legislation. The newly elected president can also issue new Executive Orders requiring presidential appointees and the rest of the new administration to adhere to strict standards with regard to upholding the Constitution and the Bill of Rights.

In addition, failure to follow the Constitution in any significant way or in any particular situation should be pointed out to the offending cabinet officer, department director or agency head for immediate correction. Failure to fix the problem in a reasonable amount of time should be just cause for their resignation or dismissal.

To facilitate upholding the Constitution, the president and the president's staff can request the resignations of all appointees from the previous administration. Of course, failure to resign would be grounds for firing. An accelerated transition team process (described later in this book) might substantially ease this reasonable effort to assure all presidential appointees are onboard with the president's effort to uphold the Constitution.

It is the sworn duty of the president, the attorney general and the administration to faithfully uphold the Bill of Rights as an integral part of upholding the Constitution. America's freedom can't be wantonly, or even casually, or even occasionally, infringed upon by government.

Religious freedom, freedom of speech, and the other freedoms guaranteed by the Constitution and the Bill of Rights must be protected for all Americans. The president must make this endeavor an ongoing goal of the administration. Making all presidential appointees aware of the need to preserve, protect and defend the Constitution will be a top priority of the new conservative president.

Violating the Separation of Powers

The separation of powers must be maintained among the three branches of government: the Executive, legislative, and judicial branches. Quite correctly, violating the separation of powers by one branch of the government is simply another instance of violating the Constitution. The Constitution clearly articulates and mandates the separation of powers. But, since it is such an egregious disregard for the Constitution and such an overt opportunity for tyranny to creep into the Federal government, it is worth calling out for special and close scrutiny.

Here again, the solution to the issue of violating the separation of powers starts with the newly elected president. The president must faithfully execute the laws under his or her watchful eyes. The president must be assisted closely with a competent and forceful attorney general that is committed to upholding the Constitution. The newly elected, comprehensive conservative president will no doubt appoint just such an attorney general.

The president and the administration should be committed to maintain a clear separation of powers, letting Congress create new laws or amend old laws, and permitting the courts to interpret the laws following the Constitution, in-place legislation, and precedent. The Supreme Court and the lower courts should concern themselves with following the original intent of the Constitution and legislation, not reading into the Constitution or into existing laws their own personal opinions, preferences, or political interpretation. The will of the people as expressed by the duly elected representatives of the people in legislation should not be circumvented by the will of Supreme Court justices or judges sitting in courts across America.

If the Supreme Court encounters previous court decisions that obviously crossed the boundaries of good Constitutional jurisprudence, they should be committed to overturning "settled law" from the past that is unconstitutional or legally inappropriate.

Lower courts need to follow the lead of the Supreme Court and adhere to a similar philosophy of judicial restraint.

Over time, the newly elected president will likely have the opportunity to appoint four or more Supreme Court justices during his or her term of office. The candidates for presidential appointments to the Supreme Court ought to be selected from a pool of outstanding lawyers, legal scholars and jurists based on their judicial record and judicial temperament. They need to align with the core principles with regard to the Constitution, the Bill of Rights and the Rule of Law. They need to address Constitutional issues, analysis and decision-making from an originalist perspective of the Constitution.

If a potential justice has no judicial track record, or doesn't hold an originalist interpretation of the Constitution, it doesn't make sense for that person to receive a presidential appointment. A Supreme Court appointment is a vitally important post in the judicial branch of our government. To move forward on an unproven judicial candidate or a candidate whose legal decisions doesn't comport with originalism is a Constitutional risk.

As alluded to earlier, Article 3 gives Congress the authority to alter the makeup of courts. One way to enforce the proper Constitutional temperament is to increase or decrease the size or scope of Federal courts. Also, the very existence of certain courts might come into question. Normal attrition (such as retirements and resignations) over time will also thin the ranks of progressive justices and judges currently on the bench.

No doubt the newly elected president will carefully screen future Supreme Court justices and lower court judges and appoint only those that will uphold the Constitution, the Bill of Rights, and the Rule of Law. Getting control of judicial appointments is a vital component to creating the new Conservative Era.

Violating the Rule of Law

One of the 12 core principles for the new Conservative Era is: "We are committed to upholding the Rule of Law." Conservative voters will expect all Federal, State and local elected officials to uphold the Rule of Law equally to all citizens. This is a given for voters, who will no longer tolerate flagrantly ignoring the Rule of Law. The disregard for the Rule of Law is one strong reason why Americans feel so much moral outrage over their government, approaching the critical presidential election of 2016.

In fact, any officeholder that fails to uphold the Rule of Law can be expected to be recalled or not re-elected to office again.

The president sets the example for upholding the Rule of Law and is a national role model for this vital Constitutional behavior. The president's administration, members of the House and Senate, Supreme Court justices and lower court judges, elected State and local officials all need to model their behavior on upholding the Rule of Law.

Indeed, upholding the Rule of Law is a basic necessity for a civilized society that operates with morality and freedom. Without upholding the Rule of Law, a nation can't have morality. The Rule of Law offers the nation true justice and equality. The Rule of Man (be it a capricious president, a party committee, or a ruthless dictator) is subject to the whim of those in power. It is the antithesis of justice and equality.

Without morality, a nation can't have freedom. Conversely, without freedom, a nation can't have morality. Morality and freedom are inextricably linked together within a free nation.[207]

Incidentally, that's why the following two statements are true. As America's morality has declined, so too, its freedom has declined. Similarly, as America's freedom has declined, so too, America's morality has declined. To illustrate the veracity of these statements, just look around America at the end of the Anti-Constitutional Era and consider the many individual examples that jump out at you within the context of your own life.

Two particular areas where the Rule of Law has not been upheld at the end of the Anti-Constitutional Era are with regard to the enforcement of our immigration laws and with regard to the implementation of ObamaCare. Both of these two instances have generated considerable angst and anxiety among Americans. The newly elected comprehensive conservative president will deal with these issues decisively.

Across the wide-ranging issues facing America, our newly elected conservative president will be an outstanding role model for, and proponent of, upholding the Rule of Law. Other appointed and elected officials will follow suit and will model the Rule of Law throughout America. The Rule of Law will once again guard both justice and equality in America.

Violating Domestic Peace – Rioting and Racial Tensions in Our Cities

The Rule of Law also means maintaining domestic peace. Our cities and towns as well as our counties and rural areas, all require domestic peace. Americans expect to live in peace.

As we pointed out earlier in this book, some progressive socialist policies and programs during the Anti-Constitutional Era have led to the encouragement of increased racial tensions, additional violence in our cities, and even destructive rioting. Instead of focusing on domestic peace, progressive socialists blame their political opponents for racial tensions in an effort to callously garner votes. Progressives might even go so far as to directly overlook crime and seemingly encourage violence by urging law enforcement to stand down at critical times.

Rather than seeking peace, progressives seek funding for future government programs. Unfortunately, the neighborhoods that live with crime, violence and even rioting are really being hurt the hardest.

Indeed, racial and ethnic minorities need first and foremost real economic opportunities, brought about by morality and freedom and the core principles of prosperity through strong economic growth. They need police protection in their neighborhoods to safely participate in the economic prosperity that the new Conservative Era will bring for all Americans.

Racial and ethnic minorities don't need or desire progressive socialist politicians emasculating the police, who are trying to protect all of our great cities and their individual neighborhoods. They don't need or desire their police to live in fear of doing their jobs. They don't need or desire their police to be criticized constantly, to be given onerous paperwork, to face unfair and over-the-top prosecutions for ordinary day-to-day police work, and to worry about the potential loss of careers and pensions.

With the dawning of the new Conservative Era, Americans of all racial and ethnic backgrounds will come together and join forces to secure our nation through a strong military, and build our nation through a vibrant, thriving economy. Through the four core principles that result in a growing economy, America will no longer settle for a lackluster, anemic and jobless recovery that constantly dangles Americans on the brink of another Great Recession, with outrageously high, inner city, teenage and minority unemployment levels.

The old progressive socialist economy based on government programs is overwhelmingly drab and dismal. It literally breaks people's spirits and discourages people's efforts, and leaves people to hopelessly live on mediocre government handouts. All of these factors amount to nothing more than spiritual decay and material subsistence.

The newly elected comprehensive conservative president will lead the charge to bring racial tensions finally into racial harmony. Hope will be based on economic opportunity and growth through traditional American values, not the growth of tangled government welfare programs, and not the grudging benevolence of progressive socialist politicians.

Domestic peace will be the result of strong economic opportunity, economic growth and widespread prosperity. Just as free trade (that is truly fair) among nations leads to world peace, economic freedom and prosperity within a nation lead to domestic peace and harmony.

The Conservative Era will see a vast reduction in rioting and racial tensions and a concomitant increase in economic opportunity, prosperity, and domestic peace.

Violating Domestic Peace – A National Crime Wave
The national crime wave we spoke of earlier in this book is another significant issue adding to the moral outrage of voters preceding the critical presidential election of 2016. Its causes and cures are similar to the points made above.

A crime wave is a reflection of the breakdown of law and order. In a sense, it is another example of the failure to uphold the Rule of Law. It simply can't be tolerated. Its likely causes stem from progressive interference in local police enforcement. Its likely cure revolves around freeing police to do their jobs.

The newly elected conservative president can enhance and empower police forces around the country to do their jobs, by requesting the attorney general and the Department of Justice (DOJ) to provide assistance when certain skill sets, technologies and assets are requested by local law enforcement officials. The attorney general and the DOJ can also reverse the heavy burdens associated with unnecessary paperwork that have blocked the police in many cities in recent years. These factors will also reduce costs to local police budgets.

Summary
We can see that the core principles of the new Conservative Era directly address the issues of morality and freedom with common sense solutions. The newly elected, comprehensive conservative president will lead the nation forward in addressing these issues with common sense solutions. In parallel, the moral outrage of Americans will diminish as they see these common sense solutions to issues implemented.

In the next Chapter, we look at common sense solutions to the issues of national security.

Chapter 10

Common Sense Solutions to the Issues of National Security

In addition to issues surrounding morality and freedom, Americans share a deep concern for issues dealing with national security. Americans are worried about a number of threats that might imminently impact our national security and affect our peace at home. We have discussed these threats earlier in this book. Let's turn our attention now to some common sense solutions to these issues of national security and peace using the core principles that guide the new Conservative Era.

The Threats Posed by America's Unprotected Borders and Illegal Immigration

Of grave concern to many Americans are our unprotected borders and illegal immigration and the host of issues surrounding these two related threats. We have explored these issues earlier. What are some common sense solutions to deal with these major threats to America?

First and foremost, to be a sovereign nation, a country must have borders and those borders must be clearly delineated and must be readily enforced. Closely related, the laws regarding immigration must be carefully followed. This is an obvious application of the core principle about upholding the Rule of Law. But, in addition, it is so fundamental that it merits its own core principle: "We are committed to maintaining Secure Borders."

One common sense solution that the newly elected conservative president can take is to completely shut down America's borders for a "cooling off period" of two years. This means no new immigrants (legal or illegal) will be permitted to enter and stay in the United States. This gives the new administration the time to seal the border off from illegal immigration completely – physically with fencing, electronically using advanced tracking technology, and militarily with appropriate law enforcement and military support, if needed.

A two year cooling off period permits the new administration to simultaneously review and reconsider all immigration laws and all related policies for a variety of vital national interests. For example, if we allow future legal immigrants into America, under what circumstances can we be assured that they are not sneaking in with terrorist intentions; or, they don't have plans to invade America and to circumvent the American Constitution with other forms of foreign law; or, they are not carrying new contagious diseases into America to infect the population.

Another assessment that the new administration can make surrounding the question of new, legal immigrants is what skill sets are required in America. Still another area is what new, legal immigrants are likely to have the abilities and capabilities to successfully integrate into our society. Integration into America is clearly preferable to the balkanization of America into spheres of isolation.

Beyond these factors, another question to consider and to formulate intelligent policy around is our humanitarian concern for potential immigrants. How many migrants should America take in for strictly humanitarian reasons? What funding level in the Federal budget should be allocated for this purpose? What funding levels can States and local governments afford? Plus, can the Federal government aid the States in this endeavor?

The newly elected, comprehensive conservative president will need to lead the nation, his or her administration, Congress, and the States to pursue and implement potential new legislation and policies that thoughtfully resolve the lingering twin problems of America's unprotected borders and illegal immigration.

The core principles of the new Conservative Era provide a smart framework for dealing with America's national security issues and ensuring our peace. Let's look next at the second big national security threat that Americans recognize and hope to eliminate from their list of serious concerns.

The Threats Posed by Potential Terrorist Attacks

We all know that this is a serious threat. But, what can be done to mitigate, and then to eliminate, this grave threat to our national security and peace?

A first important step is to speak the truth to the American people and to the world. It's imperative to identify terrorism, to acknowledge terrorism, to recognize terrorism, and to call terrorist acts precisely what they are, "terrorism."

It's also vital to alert the nation to prepare for, and guard against, terrorism. Let's educate all Americans on how to recognize potential terrorism and how to report possible threats. Let's make sure we all know how to protect ourselves, our families, our friends, our property, and our businesses.

The next critical step is to prosecute to the fullest extent possible any terrorist act that is committed against Americans.

In addition to identification, naming and recognizing terrorism, education and awareness, and prosecution, we need to prioritize the resources of the Federal government to protect the American people. Terrorism is not an idle threat. It represents a major threat to American lives, American property, and the American Economy.

The newly elected, comprehensive conservative president will lead the nation and the American military in protecting America against terrorism. Congress will likely enhance military budgets to add people and resources to meet this imminent threat. Finally, our intelligence capabilities will need to be enhanced within America and around the world. If necessary, our military might need to take the fight directly to the sources of the terrorism, and deal with it at the origin of its deadly philosophy, strategy and tactics.

It is the role of our new conservative commander-in-chief to protect our great nation and all Americans from the threats posed by potential terrorist attacks.

The Threats Posed by the Terrible Iran Nuclear Deal

As we know, the Iran nuclear deal is a terrible deal for a long list of reasons we explained earlier in this book. This deal is one more threat that has added to the palpable moral outrage American voters are bringing into the critical presidential election of 2016. What common sense solutions do our core principles bring to bear on this significant threat to our national security and peace?

The new conservative president can unilaterally declare the Iran nuclear deal as null and void in several ways. Since it was formulated as an Executive Agreement, the president can terminate it as an Executive Order. That's one direct approach the president can take.

Or, since the Executive Agreement was in reality a veiled or hidden treaty with Iran and several other nations, it was definitely unconstitutional from the start. The reason is simple. It bypassed the Constitution's treaty process that requires the advice and consent of the Senate that stipulates a two-thirds vote to pass. This cloaked treaty never received the necessary two thirds approval of the Senate. Again, the new conservative president can choose to end this covert treaty that has masqueraded as a legitimate (albeit illicit) attempt to bypass the treaty ratification process in the Constitution.

The awkward and convoluted Corker amendment that was used to garner some type of "approval optics" to hide the failure to follow the Constitution, might have been entered into with good intentions by some members of Congress. But, even this rather strange and inverted approval mechanism was not followed precisely. The Corker amendment fails on its face to add legitimacy to the Executive Agreement.[208] The Iran nuclear deal fails on all fronts to be a constitutionally approved treaty.

Expect the new conservative president to terminate the "Executive Agreement" by whatever means is best.

Next, expect the president to re-authorize economic sanctions against Iran. Because Congress didn't approve the Iran nuclear "treaty," the president will probably declare the U. N. Security Council adoption of resolution No. 2231 (2015) endorsing the Iran nuclear deal and apparently calling for the termination of both the 1696 and 1929 resolutions as non-binding on the United States.

Recall the current embargo against Iran was implemented by two U. N. Security Council resolutions: No. 1696 (2006) and No. 1929 (2010). The first bars the sale or transfer to Iran of technology related to ballistic-missiles, and the second does the same for other military equipment such as battle tanks, combat aircraft, attack helicopters, and warships.

The newly elected conservative president, while in the process of ending the terrible Iran nuclear deal, also will be cutting off additional dollars from reaching Iranian-funded terrorist organizations. This might also diminish to some extent the threat of terrorist attacks on the American people and the American homeland.

By ending the Iran nuclear deal, the newly elected conservative president will also terminate the serious threats posed by this terrible deal.

A separate, but related, set of threats to our national security and peace stem from the real threats posed by a potential Electro-Magnetic Pulse (EMP) attack on America.

The Threats Posed by a Potential Electro-Magnetic Pulse (EMP) Attack on America and the Meltdown of America's Electric Grid

An Electro-Magnetic Pulse (EMP) attack against America is one of the most devastating and horrific potential threats to America imaginable. A newly elected, comprehensive conservative president will make the protection against this threat a top priority for the new administration. What are the common sense solutions to this grave threat to America?

First, ending the terrible Iran nuclear deal will help to eliminate the possibility of Iran launching an EMP attack against America directly by itself – something mentioned earlier in this book that is endorsed in a secret Iran military textbook obtained by our military. Taking this action (that is, ending the Iran nuclear deal) also lessens the risk that Iran would give one of the terrorist groups it funds nuclear weapons and ballistic missiles to launch an EMP attack against us indirectly. The newly elected conservative president can end the Iran nuclear deal quickly as explained in the previous section.

Second, the newly elected conservative president can direct our military to immediately upgrade NORAD's Cheyenne Mountain facilities near Colorado Springs to be able to detect an inbound EMP attack from a southern trajectory, a capability that NORAD doesn't currently have to protect America.[209] *The Wall Street Journal* reported that:

> … Iran should be regarded as already having nuclear missiles capable of making an EMP attack against the U.S. Iran and North Korea have successfully orbited satellites on south-polar trajectories that appear to practice evading U.S. missile defenses, and at optimum altitudes to make a surprise EMP attack.
>
> The U.S. has no ballistic-missile early-warning radars or ground-based interceptors facing south and would be blind to a nuclear warhead orbited as a satellite from a southern trajectory. The missile defense plans were oriented during the Cold War for a northern strike from the Soviet Union, and they have not been adapted for the changing threats.[210]

This vital upgrade to NORAD must be done as soon as possible.

Third, America's electric grid can be "hardened" from an Electro-Magnetic Pulse attack at a relatively small cost. For an estimated few billion dollars, the potential loss of our national grid can be protected from an EMP attack. Unfortunately, while the House passed such legislation in recent years, it was stalled in the Senate. Apparently, the current president has also failed to act on the Congressional EMP Commission's latest unclassified report or their suggested Executive Order to defend our national infrastructure.[211] But, the newly elected, conservative president will act to protect America's electric grid.

Expect the newly elected conservative president to immediately press Congressional leadership to make our national electric grid safe with enabling legislation and funding. For the relatively few dollars involved, the massively destructive consequences of such an EMP attack can be avoided, further safeguarding Americans.

Fourth, strategically deploying weapons such as Terminal High-Altitude Area Defense (THAAD) batteries might be one reasonable and common sense approach to protecting against EMP attacks.[212]

Fifth, America can initiate advanced weapons R&D to explore prospective technologies for defending against EMP attacks. For example, one might envision roughly adapting Boeing's recently obtained patent for force field technology to offer a novel approach to dealing with systems related to EMP attacks. While using Boeing's electro-magnetic arc technology meant for anti-shockwave attacks, further R&D might result in a conceptually equivalent anti-EMP weapons technology.[213]

We need to consider, research, develop, build and deploy advanced weapons systems as they become available. The newly elected conservative president and conservative Congress should protect America with these new advanced weapons, especially considering the unstable and often hostile, global situation. Being strong is in itself a strong deterrent to war.

The newly elected conservative president, the president's military advisors, and their weapons experts can determine the best course of action to proceed in this arena. The good news is that the new president will take those actions necessary to protect the American people. These threats will no longer be ignored by an ambivalent president or stalled in Congress by partisan concerns.

All of these common sense solutions to the significant and catastrophic threats posed by an EMP attack on America and the subsequent meltdown of America's electric grid can be taken early in the new president's administration. They follow the core principle for the new Conservative Era: "We are committed to maintaining a Strong Military Defense."

The final set of threats to our national security and peace that are worrying Americans daily and are adding to the moral outrage of voters leading up to the critical presidential election of 2016 are cyber hacks, cyber attacks, and attacks on our critical infrastructure. Let's look at common sense solutions to these threats briefly.

The Threats Posed by Potential Major Cyber Hacks, Cyber Attacks, and Physical Sabotage on America's Critical Infrastructure

As discussed earlier, the threats posed by potential major cyber hacks, cyber attacks, and physical sabotage on America's critical infrastructure are far reaching. They encompass military, commercial, financial, and healthcare computer systems and information targets. Air traffic control and electric utilities are particular targets. The scope of vulnerabilities and the range of common sense solutions go far beyond what can be covered in this book.

What is important to state here is that the newly elected, comprehensive conservative president will take these threats seriously and will act accordingly. Whether it is new software and hardware technology for security perimeters around airports, or it is the regional stocking of transformers for electric utility transmission substations (for quick replacement after an attack), the new conservative president will work hard to protect America from these threats.

The core conservative principles dealing with peace through a strong military defense include not only recognizing major military attacks that are conventional or nuclear in nature, but also direct attacks on the American homeland from whatever direction they come, or in whatever form they take.

Summary

We can see that the core principles of the new Conservative Era directly address the issues of national security and peace with common sense solutions. The newly elected, comprehensive conservative president will lead the nation forward in addressing these issues with common sense solutions. In parallel, the moral outrage of Americans will diminish as they see these common sense solutions to national security issues implemented.

Americans will once again feel secure during the new Conservative Era.

In the next Chapter, we look at common sense solutions to the major issues of economic security.

Chapter 11

Common Sense Solutions to the Issues of Economic Security

Besides the paramount issues Americans sense that deal with morality and freedom as well as the vitally significant issues that deal with our national security and peace, there is one other area of deep concern to voters as we approach the critical presidential election of 2016. These issues that further fuel America's moral outrage deal with our anemic and listless economy and our lack of economic security. We have studied the issues of economic security earlier in this book. Now, let's focus our attention on intelligent, common sense solutions to these issues that will probably be implemented quickly by the newly elected, comprehensive conservative president.

Lack of Jobs and Economic Growth

At the top of the list of economic security issues facing Americans today is the lack of good jobs and the lack of economic growth across the economy. Just as then Senator John F. Kennedy said in 1960: "… a rising tide lifts all boats,"[214] it's true that a falling tide lowers all boats. Americans are rightfully frustrated, angry and upset with the state of the economy preceding the critical presidential election of 2016.

Indeed, America has never fully recovered from the Great Recession, despite attempts by the progressive socialists in government and their willing mainstream media accomplices to paint a rosy picture of the economy to the contrary. Americans are practical, have common sense, and can pick up the accurate economic signals in their own lives that tell the true story.

America needs more jobs, not just for college graduates with large college loan balances to pay off, but also for managers and employees that have been downsized, or have been "excessed" as some might call it, or have experienced a "RIF" (Reduction in Force). Quite possibly, they are among the countless Americans with part time jobs that want "more hours" and higher pay by working more time in their current jobs. Or, they want to use their education, experience, knowledge and skills more fully, but are currently "under-employed" taking whatever job that they can get at the moment.

Americans have seen the lackluster pace of the economy in down-to-earth practical terms – higher prices for many items such as healthcare, food and housing. But, no concomitant increases in their paychecks, assuming they have a paycheck and are not living on their severance pay, their savings, their unemployment benefits, their welfare benefits, or their food stamps. Of course, many are living on government benefits because they are unable to find a good job and have been forced into the world of government Electronic Benefits Transfer (EBT).[215]

Jobs, Productivity and Economic Growth are Needed Now. One principle of economics is worth emphasizing in this discussion. Economic growth is dependent upon two factors, both of which our common sense solutions below will address. To achieve significant and sustained economic growth, we need growth in the number of jobs in America and we need growth in overall productivity.[216]

We have discussed the lack of jobs already. But, how is America doing in terms of productivity today?

At the present time, under progressive government programs and policies, productivity has been running at only about 50% of its historical rate.[217] Is it any wonder why our economy seems anemic and stalled?

There is a pronounced lack of jobs. There is also a considerable lack of growth in productivity. Obviously, there is a prolonged inability to recover fully from the Great Recession (an economic event caused in large part by progressive socialist policies as well).

There is a palpable lack of economic growth across the entire American Economy.

Jobs, productivity, economic growth are all tied closely together. For a thriving economy, we want to empower the economy to increase all three simultaneously.

Increasing the quantity and quality of jobs significantly will directly meet the needs of millions of Americans for new employment or better employment. Indeed, millions upon millions of Americans will be able to go back to work for the first time in years. Opportunities will be abundant again. In addition, increasing the quantity and quality of jobs lays the foundation for productivity enhancements that will further boost economic growth and the incomes of millions of Americans.

Now, let's look at the core conservative principles. What do they offer us in the way of guidance to create this vital economic growth, and to re-build and to re-energize the American Economy? What common sense solutions should we follow to succeed?

Here are the four common sense solutions the new conservative president and Congress will likely take to jumpstart the American Economy.

Implement Pro-Growth Tax Policies. First, the newly elected conservative president will lead Congress in developing a pro-growth tax plan.

Some of the features of that plan will likely include cutting marginal tax rates on personal income taxes to spur the economy in two ways. Keeping more of their hard-earned money in the pockets of consumers will increase spending on both everyday goods and services (consumable goods) as well as on durable goods (things that last for years like cars and appliances). In addition, some of that money will also be saved and invested, keeping more capital in the private sector for additional savings, investment, and wealth creation for the nation.

Private sector investments generally have a higher value to the economy than government spending because the velocity of money (that is, how quickly money moves throughout the economy) is greater and because the actual money is more wisely invested in meeting the needs of both consumers and businesses. Government programs are well known for waste and failure. High visibility achievements in innovation and productivity tend to be associated with the private sector as countless examples show us.

Lowering America's excessively high corporate tax rates (as compared to the rest of the world) will also benefit the economy by giving corporations additional money for hiring more employees and by giving corporations additional money for investing in new productivity tools for employees. The results of this change in tax policy will be more jobs in America immediately, and higher paying jobs for employees in the near future as higher productivity kicks into action.

Note that higher productivity is a plus for the economy because it means employees are producing more for every hour worked on average. With additional revenues, corporations have the money to pay for needed additional employees and to fuel their own growth. They are also willing to pay higher salaries and wages to employees because they see the economic tide rising across the economy. Another factor is that with increasing economic growth, comes higher demand and pay for potential new employees as well as current employees. It's win – win – win. It's a win for employees. It's a win for businesses. It's a win for the American Economy.

Other potential pro-growth tax policies will likely be considered by the new conservative president and Congress, including a completely flat tax at a lower marginal tax rate than current rates; cuts in, or elimination of, capital gains taxes; and the elimination of the net investment income tax (NIIT). The NIIT was put into place by the ObamaCare law in 2010[218] and is also sometimes called the 3.8% Medicare surtax on investment income.[219] Eliminating the estate tax (or death tax as it is also called) is another positive tax policy for the nation.

There are other pro-growth tax policies that will spur more growth and more jobs for America. Of course, they require amending the tax code. We won't attempt to go into the detail of many of those potential improvements in the tax code in this venue, preferring instead to provide this higher level summary of major pro-growth tax policies.

You can expect the new conservative president and Congress to quickly put into place a comprehensive pro-growth tax plan that will rapidly accelerate and grow the American Economy. This is the first common sense solution to the issues of lack of jobs and lack of economic growth in America. What's the next common sense solution?

Implement Pro-Growth Spending Policies. Second, the newly elected conservative president will lead the Congress in developing pro-growth spending policies that align better with both national needs and anticipated revenues. In developing a pro-growth budget the president and Congress will probably employ dynamic modeling (vs. the less accurate static models of the past). The economic goal of a long term stable economy means the spending plan will strive to eliminate on-going deficit spending and out-of-control and mounting Federal debt.

Implementing pro-growth tax policies and spending policies are two smart common sense solutions to the issue of a lack of jobs and economic growth in the American Economy. What is the third common sense solution we get from our core principles of the new Conservative Era?

Implement Pro-Growth Regulatory Policies. Third, the new conservative president will work with Congress to substantially unburden the economy from the morass and plethora of government regulations. Sunset provisions can be worked into new legislation and added into existing statutes that will end regulations that are excessively costly, excessively burdensome, and that substantially hinder economic growth and new business creation. A reasonable economic goal here is to cut excessive regulations by 50% in four years.

Incidentally, in one 2014 study of regulatory costs, it was estimated that regulations cost the American Economy almost 12% of our

GDP.[220] That borders on massive economic wastefulness.

Yes, some regulations are vital to safety and health. Yes, some regulations offer comfort and assistance. Yes, some regulations are helpful or beneficial. But, 12% of GDP is too much. It literally stifles economic growth. It would be great for the economy to cut that down to 6% of GDP in four years. We can expect an enormous surge in productivity and a giant boost in economic growth and actual GDP from that factor alone!

Next, let's look at the fourth and final common sense solution to the issue of lack of jobs and economic growth in the American Economy.

Implement Pro-Growth Monetary Policies. Fourth, the new conservative president can appoint new members to the Federal Reserve that will stop following the unconventional policies of qualitative easing and ZIRP (Zero Interest Rate Policy). These Fed policies have hindered the robust recovery our economy should have had since the Great Recession. Indeed, very low interest rates have repeatedly failed to provide the economic growth the Federal Reserve thought they would produce.[121]

In addition, the Federal regulation of the quantity of credit tends to distort credit markets and misallocates capital. Consider this dramatic data from the Federal Reserve. Over approximately the last five years, total credit in the United States grew about $7.6 trillion. Of that amount, it was allocated as follows: government received $4.7 trillion, corporations $1.9 trillion, and small businesses and households received a meager $1 trillion of the $7.6 trillion.[222]

Unfortunately, the job creation powerhouse and the economic growth jet engine of a free economy is the small business portion of the private sector. Small businesses have been starved for capital for growth, thereby limiting job creation and economic growth.

According to Gallup, for about the first time in 35 years, the number of new American businesses created is less than the number of American businesses shutting down. Currently, only

400,000 new American businesses are starting up annually versus 475,000 American businesses that are closing up. Gallup also points out that America is only ranked 12th in new business creation in the world among nations.[223]

These dismal numbers can certainly be traced to the lack of capital available to small businesses. Other contributing factors, of course, include the overall regulatory burden in general, the ObamaCare regulatory burden in particular, specific regulations, etc.

In place of the failed Fed monetary policies, the newly elected conservative president and Congress can promote pro-growth monetary policies. Plus, the new conservative president can appoint members to the Federal Reserve that will implement traditional monetary policy with a proven track record of results. For example, the well-known Taylor Rule that bases interest rates on a straight-forward function of the inflation rate and GDP will likely be central to the new monetary prescriptions of the Federal Reserve during the Conservative Era.[224]

Following pro-growth monetary policies means America will almost certainly have a much more stable money supply and our dollar will have a more constant value as well. Monetary stability is a critical factor in maintaining a stable economy that empowers economic growth. It also helps strengthen the global economy and our trading partners as well.

Taken together, the implementation of pro-growth tax policies, pro-growth spending policies, pro-growth regulatory policies, and pro-growth monetary policies are common sense solutions to the lack of jobs and lack of economic growth experienced by so many Americans leading up to the critical presidential election of 2016. Taken together, they will lead to millions of new and better jobs, higher productivity and incomes, stronger economic growth, a robust economy, and a solid economic future for America.

Let's next look at the second economic security issue generating moral outrage prior to the critical presidential election of 2016 and some common sense solutions to resolving it.

Disastrous Effects of ObamaCare

As we know, ObamaCare is an economic, medical, health insurance, and practical failure. Socialized medicine, and this is a major step toward single-payer socialized medicine, is always a failure. What are some common sense solutions to dealing effectively with ObamaCare?

Simple. First, repeal ObamaCare in full.

The newly elected, conservative president will likely send to Congress a short bill repealing ObamaCare in its entirety. The conservative Congress will probably pass that legislation quickly and the new president will almost certainly sign it.

Second, and separately, expect the new conservative president and Congress to develop new legislation to deregulate the healthcare insurance market and the healthcare market to empower free market forces. This will permit innovative, lower cost, healthcare and healthcare insurance options. New solutions at a variety of reasonable price points for individuals and families, small businesses, and large corporations will most likely result.

In fact, the so-called healthcare crisis (that supposedly existed prior to ObamaCare) exaggerated the problems in the healthcare industry that were caused in large measure by government progressive socialist tax policies and regulatory policies.[225] Rather than fixing those problems in 2010 with free market principles, progressives chose instead to attempt a takeover of most of the healthcare insurance and healthcare industries. ObamaCare was the awful result causing undue hardship and confusion to millions of Americans, and adding incredible uncertainty to personal and business budgeting decisions, increasing healthcare premiums and healthcare costs, and creating a giant roadblock for new business creation and new job creation.

The beginning of the new Conservative Era will probably see ObamaCare finally repealed in full, and free market empowerment brought to both the healthcare and the healthcare insurance industries.

Thus, the disastrous effects of ObamaCare will likely be eliminated by the new conservative president and Congress by the simple repeal of the ObamaCare law that Americans were against since its enactment in 2010.

How do the core principles of the new Conservative Era help us deal with the remaining two issues of economic security?

Out-of-Control Government Spending and National Debt

The issue of out-of-control spending and soaring national debt is tackled directly by our core principles. According to our core principles, "We are committed to Pro-Growth Spending Policies." Following that principle, the Federal budget will be managed more effectively, budget deficits will gradually be brought under control by the new conservative president and Congress, and the runaway increases in national debt will stop.

Implementing pro-growth spending policies means developing common sense solutions to the Federal budgeting process and the actual Federal budget itself. It means cutting out waste in as many places as possible in the budget. You might respond: "Of course, they all say that and nothing ever happens." True.

But, for the newly elected, conservative president and the Congress, this is not wishful thinking or vague platitudes. Tough decisions on spending will almost certainly be made. Real cuts in the Federal budget will take place. Some lobbyists will be completely disappointed. Some interest groups will be decidedly upset. But, America's economic future and America's economic security are quite literally at stake.

Implementing pro-growth spending policies might also mean utilizing innovative spending reduction strategies such as the "Penny Plan," also known as the "One Cent Solution." This approach is simple and powerful. With the One Cent Solution, the government cuts one cent of every dollar it spends for everything, except interest, for each year for five years. The government also caps Federal spending at 18% of national income. This plan results in a savings of $7.5 trillion in 10 years and a balanced budget by 2019.[226]

Incidentally, with pro-growth policies, comes increasing GDP growth. That growth, in turn, will fuel more revenues into the Treasury and will make balancing the Federal budget much easier to achieve. With prosperity, the economic goals can actually happen ahead of schedule.

That's one reason too why dynamic modeling is necessary in economic planning. It gives decision-makers a better and more accurate assessment of future economic growth.

Let's look next at the fourth issue dealing with economic security.

Excessive Regulation of the American Economy

Once again, our core principles shine a bright light on intelligent, common sense solutions to this issue facing America. One of our core principles deals with the regulatory morass Americans face across our nation today: "We are committed to Pro-Growth Regulatory Policies."

We already know that regulations impede and throttle back the economy. That's a serious matter. But, sometimes it is also funny to stand back and look at many specific regulations in the context of their actual usage. Even though you often think the government has created a particularly foolish regulation, the government always seems to be able to outdo itself. Consider the next example.

The Wall Street Journal reported on a new medical coding system for diagnostic codes that healthcare providers are required to use starting October 1, 2015. Called ICD-10, the International Statistical Classification of Diseases and Related Health Problems (10th Revision) was developed by the World Health Organization and adopted by the Centers for Medicare and Medicaid Services (CMS).[227]

The rationale for ICD-10 is presumably that more precision in diagnostic codes will result in better charting and more accurate and therefore lower, reimbursement for healthcare services. Uniformity in coding can make sense. However, this system adds complexity to healthcare.

The new coding system provides doctors with about 70,000 different possible diagnostic codes! According to *The Wall Street Journal*,

> It includes such useful codes as "Struck by a duck," "Bizarre personal appearance," "Sucked into a jet engine," "Accident while knitting or crocheting" and "Burn due to water-skis on fire."

Really? Are these codes for real?

Yes, these are some of the 70,000 or so different medical conditions that ER doctors, medical specialists and family practitioners alike can use when filling in their healthcare paperwork. How many patients do you think that emergency room doctors see each year for some of these strange and unusual medical diagnoses? It's hard to image there are many patients who get "struck by a duck." It's hard to imagine these codes are reasonable or necessary. Did the government ever think this might be a bit over the top? Or, a potential waste of time for busy doctors, who need to see many patients every day?

Obviously, the regulatory mess needs to be cleaned up and will be by the new conservative president and Congress.

As was mentioned earlier in the Chapter, the new conservative president will work with Congress to substantially unburden the economy from the morass and plethora of government regulations. This issue on the minds of many voters can be overcome. Cutting the regulatory burden by 50% will increase our freedom and our prosperity in incredible ways.

Summary
Fortunately, the newly elected conservative president will likely formulate a rock solid economic program for the nation based on

decades of economic research and studies that clearly show that our core principles are highly effective in stimulating economic growth. In fact, a rising tide will lift all boats, and all lives, as well as our standard of living, and our prosperity.

Make no mistake about it. The evidence is incontrovertible. The core principles of the new Conservative Era, when implemented by the new conservative president and Congress, will lead to an enormous growth in the quantity and quality of jobs, and to an unprecedented prosperity. Following those same principles will lead to the repeal of ObamaCare as unnecessary government regulations that hinder the quality of healthcare and impede the economy.

While developing common sense solutions to our issues of economic security, the core principles will guide us to eliminate out-of-control government spending and will help America to stop recklessly increasing the national debt.

Finally, implementing pro-growth regulatory policies will deal with the bad effects of the excessive regulation of the American Economy, an issue helping to fuel the moral outrage of American voters.

In the next two Chapters, we explore election dynamics and election results for the critical presidential election of 2016.

Part V

Important FAQs (Frequently Asked Questions)

Chapter 12

Election Dynamics

This Chapter and the next Chapter answer FAQs (Frequently Asked Questions) about election dynamics and election results respectively. The last two predictions of this book are also included in these Chapters.

Here are the FAQs on election dynamics.

What are the Two Most Important Things a Citizen Can Do in an Election?

Given the moral outrage of citizens prior to the critical presidential election of 2016, many citizens will become active voters. In fact, as mentioned earlier, I predict there will be a record-setting voter turnout in 2016.

For those concerned with America's future, I think there are two important things to do. First, citizens should do their own research on the candidates, study their ideological views, and read their actual policy positions. Second, citizens should vote for the candidates that best align with their own views and policy preferences.

How Can a Citizen Tell if a Self-Proclaimed "Conservative" Candidate Will Actually Act Like a Conservative if Elected?

In recent years, many voters have been frustrated, upset and angry because they voted for candidates that portrayed themselves and their views as conservative, but failed to take conservative positions on various issues when in office.

The best way for a citizen to determine if a self-proclaimed candidate is truly conservative is not to listen to one speech during the heat of an election race and not to listen to one sound bite on a 30-second TV ad. Rather instead, a citizen should look at a candidate's long term record on several issues. Are they usually conservative? Are they conservative on most issues, most of the time? Or, do their views and policy positions vary all over the map?

Another way to assess a candidate for political office is their overall level of being conservative. We discussed this point earlier when we covered the topic of core principles for the new Conservative Era.

Consider these twin questions. Is a candidate a "cafeteria conservative" that picks and chooses what conservative positions he or she takes? Or, is the candidate a "comprehensive conservative" that endorses and adheres to all 12 core principles of the new Conservative Era?

Obviously, a comprehensive conservative will probably live out their core principles better than a cafeteria conservative, if elected to office.

How Can a Citizen Help to Eliminate Voter Fraud?

Ideally, in a free nation, all voters would be honest and no voter fraud would ever take place. In reality, some voter fraud seems to take place because some candidates or their supporters seek power over principle. That's unfortunate, of course.

One pro-active approach for a citizen to take is to volunteer as an election worker, poll watcher, election judge, or comparable position on Election Day. Some positions might even pay a small stipend for the work involved. To obtain such a job on Election Day, a citizen might need to contact their county election officials or a local political party long before the actual election.

For those not involved in the election process formally, they can still be alert while voting themselves.

If a citizen, for example, observes what appears to be voter fraud or highly suspicious behavior or is intimidated themselves while voting during an election, they can report the incident to a number of people. Certainly, it makes sense to report the activity to local poll watchers, election judges, election officials, and/or police officers on the scene.

If the initial contact does not rectify the situation, a citizen can report the incident to the county election staff, who are officiating the election. Obviously, the police department or sheriff's office might be an appropriate contact as well.

In some flagrant cases, a citizen might even choose to contact the secretary of state or the attorney general for their State.

If the citizen believes the incident is of sufficient merit and can't get satisfaction from other attempts to address the situation, contacting local or national news media including TV, radio and newspapers is another avenue to deal with the incident encountered by the citizen.

Citizens can make a difference in upholding the Rule of Law simply by aiding authorities when they identify suspicious activity. Reporting probable voter fraud is similar to notifying airport officials when a citizen sees an abandoned package at an airport, or if they are shopping and they see an apparent robbery in progress. It's good to be alert and it's good to notify authorities, who are responsible for upholding the law.

Will We See the End of the Mainstream Media's Influence (as we know it) in Presidential Elections?

To answer this question, let's first look at what constitutes the "mainstream media" as we have known it over the last few decades, and up until the recent past.

Traditionally, the mainstream media (MSM) consisted of the three major TV networks, ABC, CBS and NBC; the major newspapers including *The New York Times, The Washington Post,* and some other big city and smaller city newspapers; the major news magazines such as *Time, Newsweek*, and some other news magazines. Added to this list, the mainstream media also included other publications and media sources that followed the editorial point of view and frequently took their lead from the major TV networks, major newspapers, and major news magazines.

Note that the mainstream media generally followed a monolithic, left-wing, liberal point of view for years. This approach articulated a consistent liberal bias for ideas they promoted and against ideas that reflected more traditional values. Then, the MSM morphed into media with a decidedly progressive and socialist outlook.

Most recently, a subtle, but profound, change occurred within the MSM itself. Once priding itself on objectivity, the so-called fourth estate no longer appears to be a proponent for journalistic standards, or a watchdog for questionable political and government activities. Instead, in recent years, it seems to have evolved from an objective news source, to a biased source of left wing news, to a consistently progressive slant, to finally, a perceived "reality" that gives voice to ideologically-based "narratives."

In fact, leading up to the critical presidential election of 2016, the mainstream media apparently is a mouthpiece for "socialist narratives" seeking to aid in the transformation of America into some form of progressive socialist, socialist, Marxist, or communist government. Truth and objectivity have been clearly replaced with grossly exaggerated or non-factual narratives that support their socialist ideology.

The Decline in the Mainstream Media's Influence. It's clear that the business model of the MSM has been breaking down in recent years as well. Loss of listeners, loss of readers, loss of trust in the content … all have resulted in loss of revenues and profits. Remember, most MSM outlets are businesses that require revenues and profits to stay afloat, unless of course, someone subsidizes their activities. As listeners and readers have left the MSM, so too, advertisers have fled the MSM.

Various MSM businesses have been forced to lay off staff, a definite sign of trouble and typically imminent decline as well. Consider, for example, some examples of buyouts and layoffs that have hit the MSM. These include: *The New York Times*,[230] *Los Angeles Times*,[231]*The Boston Globe*[232] and others.

Clearly, the American people reject much in the MSM, its ideology, and its narratives. In story after story, MSM narratives are debunked for all their factual inaccuracies. Take Ferguson as a recent example. The associated false narrative has been explained numerous times by objective reports in the new media. The Ferguson narrative was blatant hypocrisy.[233]

In a free nation, citizens, who are also consumers at the same time, vote with their pocketbooks. The immediate reason for the end of the mainstream media as we know it is that most Americans reject the MSM. Hence, listenership and readership decline. Therefore, the MSM businesses decline in tandem and their previous monopoly on the news ends.

I believe there is now a critical mass of factors in place. The end of the mainstream media as we know it is taking place prior to the critical presidential election of 2016. In light of that change, the MSM will no longer have the level of influence on the presidential election they formerly had.

Of course, all the MSM businesses might not close. But, the so-called "mainstream" media will no longer be "main" stream in the sense of having extensive and primary influence over the electorate. If I might borrow from the words of Ronald Reagan, the mainstream media will be effectively banished to the "ash heap of history."[234] New, more powerful and pervasive media will spring up in its place.

In place of the MSM, Americans will seek out and obtain most of their news from the emerging new media and social media, including Talk Radio. Some might not think of Talk Radio as a new media, as radio technology itself has been around for about a hundred years. But, it is.

Rush Limbaugh began his pioneering conservative, national Talk Radio show less than three decades ago in the Anti-Constitutional Era. That means it qualifies as a potentially disruptive political communications technology leading up to, and empowering in part, the new Conservative Era.[235]

In retrospect now, Talk Radio definitely qualifies as a disruptive technology with literally thousands of Talk Radio programs across America, most of which present conservative discussions on a wide range of news issues and topics.[236]

Election conversations that genuinely move voters will take place in these emerging media. Trust will no longer be bestowed upon a story by reason of its appearance in the MSM. Rather, new trusted media sources will develop among citizens as well as voters in the new Conservative Era.

Just as the pamphlet, the newspaper, the mass circulation press, and television were the disruptive "technologies" of their day and they ushered in new American Constitutional Eras; so too, the new media, social media and Talk Radio are the disruptive technologies of today. They are largely facilitating the new Conservative Era.

Prediction #9

I believe America will witness the end of the mainstream media's influence (as we know it) on presidential elections. That's a bold statement. Yet, I believe we are at a significant inflection point in American History. Years from now, when historians look back, I believe it will be considered the time when the 20th century mainstream media died and its political influence largely collapsed. It will be considered a major turning point in American History, both in political and economic American History.

I also believe the usual influence of the mainstream media on presidential debates between the two major party candidates will diminish dramatically in 2016. It's also possible those customary quadrennial presidential debates among the major candidates will not take place at all, because Americans recognize the overt bias of the mainstream media or because one or both major candidates prefer to opt out and address the American people more directly through the new disruptive technologies.

Chapter 13

Election Results

This Chapter presents the FAQs (Frequently Asked Questions) about the election results. Specifically, it provides information on the presidential transition process and how quickly we can expect the conservative election mandate to take effect throughout the government. It also presents the tenth and final prediction in this book.

Here are the FAQs on election results.

How to Accelerate the New President's Transition Team?

To address the moral outrage of voters as soon as possible and to start implementing solutions to the nation's pressing challenges, the newly elected conservative president will need to take action immediately upon taking office. To state the obvious, there is much work for the new president to accomplish, and it must begin right away.

The Transition Timeframe. An important component of that massive effort is the president-elect's Transition Team and the transition plans and processes that prepare for the actual transition. A subset of the Transition Team is the "Day One Team" that makes in-depth action plans for the president on Inauguration Day. Of course, according to the Twentieth Amendment to the Constitution, the actual transition itself from one president and their administration to the new president and their administration for the critical presidential election of 2016 takes place at noon on January 20th. For the critical presidential election of 2016, that translates into noon Eastern Time on January 20th, 2017.

The real transition, however, is a complex and arduous process that extends well beyond the Inauguration Day ceremonies and festivities. In addition, it doesn't just start on the day after Election Day and continue up until Inauguration Day on January 20th, 2017. It needs to start much earlier than Election Day and it lasts months into the new administration.

Presidential Transition Laws. Before answering the question about how to accelerate the new president's transition team, it's worth understanding (at least at a high level) the legislation already in place to facilitate a successful presidential transition. No attempt is made to give a complete and thorough description of existing presidential transition law, rather only a rough discussion of the subject.

The President Transition Act of 1963 (Public Law 88-277) authorizes the Federal government's General Services Administration (GSA) to provide for a president-elect and vice president-elect the following types of administrative support: office staff compensation, office space, furniture, office equipment, supplies, travel expenses, car rentals, printing, etc. It also authorizes GSA to pay for services from experts, consultants and organizations to support the transition.

The Pre-Election Presidential Election Act of 2010 (Public Law 111-283) authorizes help for eligible presidential candidates starting within three business days of the last major party nominating convention. It does have a provision for a third party candidate that is deemed eligible too. It means that presidential transition planning can commence after the major party conventions are concluded and the major party candidates are known.

The Pre-Election Presidential Election Act of 2010 also authorized a "transition coordinating council composed of high-level executive branch officials selected by the president"[237] to aid the new president and his future administration.

Other legislation has been considered recently by the Homeland Security and Government Affairs Committee in the United States Senate to improve the transition process.[238] To the extent possible, best practices and advanced security approaches need to be adopted on a bipartisan basis to protect America during the next presidential transition process.

High Performance, High Velocity Transition Team. In addition to all the legislative efforts in place or potentially to become enacted soon, the newly elected conservative president will need a high performance, high velocity Transition Team. It's imperative that this team actually be in place prior to Election Day and that it mirrors the efforts of the Federal government to foster a smooth transition. This is a complex and convoluted challenge at best that requires state-of-the-art leadership and management processes, systems, tools and apps. It must be led by a select team of the best and brightest in America.

Let's consider how this Transition Team can accelerate its work by outstanding organization and planning, and by creating an exceptionally robust knowledge base. An in-depth analysis of Transition Team efforts is beyond the scope of this book; but, a few insights might be of interest here.

Because the Federal government has grown so large and complex, a knowledge base must be created along about seven distinct dimensions: (1) departments and agencies; (2) policies, policy levers, and policy decisions; (3) existing relationships, communications systems, computer systems and networks; (4) on-going security and newly identified, enhanced security; (5) current staffing, new staffing, and personnel management; (6) cross-functional, cross-agency, legislative, and judicial imperatives; and (7) national security and economic security requirements, upgrades and enhancements.

In addition, a complete array of technology solutions should be put in place to support the transition team, its plans, processes, and efforts.

A particular challenge to the new conservative president and administration are political appointments. People make an enormous difference in implementing policy decisions efficiently and effectively. It's important to get the right people, in the right jobs, tasked with the right policy directives, within the Federal government.

According to the Government Accountability Office (GAO), in 2012 there were a remarkable 3,799 political Federal appointments, divided up among four specific categories: (1) Presidential Appointments with Senate Confirmations (PAS); (2) Presidential Appointments without Senate Confirmations (PAs); (3) political appointments to the Senior Executive Service (SES); and (4) Schedule C political appointments.[239]

What's the difference between the four groups of political appointments? The PAS group includes "cabinet agency secretaries and top administrators and deputy administrators of the non-cabinet agencies." They carry out the president's goals and policies. The PAs generally cover appointments to the staff that work under members of the PAS group of high level administrators. Senior Executive Service appointments are essentially high level leaders and managers that oversee the Federal workforce across about 75 different Federal agencies. Finally, Schedule C appointments represent political appointments to such jobs as regional directors, speech writers, and staff assistants.[240]

Transition Team Leadership and Acceleration. Selecting the leaders of the Transition Team is a vital task for both the acceleration and the overall success of the presidential transition. Here are some principles the newly elected president can follow in overseeing the transition.

First, it's helpful to designate the leaders early and quietly. It's important not to distract the campaign in progress from the transition that openly swings into action on the day after Election Day. What's needed is a tough-minded focus on getting the right staffing in place. For example, Reagan's long-term aide, Edwin Meese III, was chosen by Reagan to be the transition director before the election. His criteria for seeking out potential cabinet appointments were: (1) philosophical commitment to Reagan; (2) integrity; (3) competence; (4) tough-mindedness; and (5) team player. Meese communicated these factors to E. Pendleton James, an executive search expert, early in the process.[241]

For the Transition Team itself, president-elect Reagan had three leaders answering directly to him. They were Edwin Meese III, the Transition Team director, who would become Counselor to the President with cabinet rank; James A. Baker III, Reagan's chief of staff; and Michael K. Deaver, deputy chief of staff. Two key people reported directly to Meese: Richard Allen (National Security Assistant) and Martin Anderson (Domestic Policy Adviser). Deaver handled scheduling and troubleshooting among other responsibilities.[242]

Second, be humble.[243] Yet, be confident in God's guidance in the same way as William McKinley was in his First Inaugural Address:

> In obedience to the will of the people, and in their presence, by the authority vested in me by this oath, I assume the arduous and responsible duties of President of the United States, relying upon the support of my countrymen and invoking the guidance of Almighty God. Our faith teaches that there is no safer reliance than upon the God of our fathers, who has so singularly favored the American people in every national trial, and who will not forsake us so long as we obey His commandments and walk humbly in His footsteps.[244]

Being humble and yet, being confident is a principle that might seem difficult for some to follow. But, the transition is a particularly complex process with ample opportunities for making mistakes. Staying humble opens up the president-elect and staff members to listen to ideas from the old administration's staff members, career appointees, and to new friends from within the campaign they are just now meeting for the first time.[245] Gaining knowledge and insights from others in this difficult endeavor can be instrumental in accelerating the process and its likelihood of success without major problems.

Being humble, of course, does not mean being asleep during the transition. The president-elect's staff needs to be aware of, and quickly recognize, those who might not philosophically support the newly elected, conservative president's philosophy. Philosophical commitment to the new president-elect is critical to policy implementation and to the development of the common sense solutions that voters seek.

Third, the new president needs to establish "clear lines of authority" that flow directly from the president to the staff and to others down the chain of command.[246] Closely related to communicating clear lines of authority, the new president must also establish strategic leadership, management and policy objectives and designate precise responsibilities for accomplishing those objectives. Clear communication of the lines of authority, objectives, and responsibilities are essential for the president and his top level staff. Further, accurate communications down the chain of command need to be accomplished by the senior leadership and management staff.

Developing Transition Team leadership early and quietly and following the above principles will likely lead to an accelerated and successful transition.

To sum up, the comprehensive conservative presidential candidate will probably begin the presidential transition process during the actual campaign by forming and leading a high performance, high velocity presidential Transition Team. Following the principles outlined above will also help to accelerate the transition process. You can expect that the Transition Team's efforts will be greatly accelerated over previous transitions due to better organization, planning, processes, technology, leadership and motivation to fix the vital issues facing America.

The newly elected conservative president will also lead the actual final transition efforts starting on January 20th, 2017.

How Fast Will it Take …

After the critical presidential election of 2016 and the accelerated work of the high performance, high velocity presidential Transition Team is complete or nearly complete, Americans want to see election results fast. The voters want answers to questions like: "How fast will the illegal immigration problem get solved?" or "How fast will the economy rebound again?" or "How fast before we will see strong job growth once again?"

Let's dive in and try to answer these FAQs.

To Repeal Obama's Executive Orders? During the transition process, the Day One Team will put together an Executive Order for the new conservative president to sign after the swearing-in ceremony and Inaugural Address. Most likely, the new president will go inside the Capitol immediately after the Inauguration and sign an Executive Order repealing many previous Executive Orders that are deemed to be inappropriate for Constitutional, legal or policy reasons. The new president will then go on to the Inaugural Luncheon.

How fast will it take to repeal Obama's Executive Orders? The answer is about 15 minutes after the actual Inauguration Ceremony concludes and immediately preceding the Inaugural Luncheon.

To Repeal Obama's Iran Nuclear Executive Agreement? As discussed earlier in this book, the new conservative president likely has several good approaches for nullifying the terrible Iran Nuclear Executive Agreement. Since it was never formulated as a treaty among nations and the Senate never ratified it as a treaty, it's essentially an Executive Order. The new president can terminate it quickly by signing a separate Executive Order declaring the previously signed Iran Nuclear Executive Agreement to be completely null and void.

How fast will it take to repeal Obama's Iran Nuclear Executive Agreement? The answer is about five minutes after repealing Obama's other questionable and problematic Executive Orders. That terrible deal should end soon after both the Presidential Oath of Office is administered and the Inaugural Address is delivered.

To Secure Our Borders? I envision a potential three step process to secure America's borders. During Step 1, the new president will order the Secretary of the U. S. Department of Homeland Security and the Commissioner of U. S. Customs and Border Protection (along with its roughly 60,000 employees) to immediately secure our borders to the extent possible, using all existing resources currently available.

To complete the task of border security and in parallel with this imminent action, the new president will also direct the Secretary to develop within 90 days, an even more complete, Comprehensive National Border Security Plan (CNBSP) detailing precise steps as well as resources and funding necessary to get the job done.

During Step 1, if the Secretary believes a national emergency exists, the new president can also order the military to protect our borders, to restore peace and order, and to secure our borders adequately, until the Department of Homeland Security gets up to speed.

If necessary, Step 2 will include Congressional hearings, debate, and the possible, fast track passage of any appropriate legislation that the president and Congress deem to be required. Target date for passage of any such legislation and the presidential signature might be July 4, 2017.

If necessary, Step 3 is the implementation of any new border security legislation. The target goal might be complete ocean-to-ocean border security by July 4, 2018.

How fast will it take to secure our borders? If the above scenario plays out, the answer is approximately 18 months from Inauguration Day through complete ocean-to-ocean border security, with Step 1 being taken on Inauguration Day, and Step 2 complete in less than six months.

To Repeal ObamaCare? In a parallel fashion, repealing the bureaucratic complexity of ObamaCare is in my view a three step process that will take about 18 months to fully repeal and replace with free market processes and sufficient economic freedom to empower America to once again have a great healthcare insurance industry and the best healthcare system in the world.

As in the case of border security, during Step 1, the president will order the appropriate Secretary, in this case the Secretary of Health and Human Services, to immediately begin planning for the orderly repeal and replacement of ObamaCare. The president also will probably order the Secretary to take whatever steps possible to unwind ObamaCare while any potential legislative package is being written and passed.

The presidential order in Step 1 also will likely require the Secretary to lead the administration's efforts to develop a Comprehensive Healthcare Freedom and Innovation Plan (CHFIP) that includes: (1) the full repeal of ObamaCare; (2) the replacement of ObamaCare with policies and processes that empower freedom of choice among patients, doctors, hospitals, and others; (3) the deregulation of the healthcare insurance industry to meet the needs and budgets of consumers and businesses, by providing a variety of plans with different benefit packages at different price points; and (4) the freedom of the healthcare industry to compete, to lower costs, and to innovate with new drugs, new medical procedures, and new medical devices.

Step 2 will probably include Congressional hearings, debate, and the potential fast track passage of any appropriate legislation that the president and Congress deem to be required to completely replace ObamaCare and to empower both the healthcare insurance industry and our healthcare system. Target date for passage of any such legislation and the presidential signature might again be about July 4, 2017.

Step 3 will likely be the implementation of any new healthcare legislation that is passed by Congress and signed into law by the new conservative president. The target goal might be a reinvigorated free market in healthcare insurance and an empowered healthcare system by July 4, 2018.

How fast will it take to repeal ObamaCare? The answer is about 18 months after Inauguration Day taking an approach similar to the one outlined above. That accomplishment includes replacing ObamaCare with consumer freedom, healthcare provider freedom, free market innovations, and less expensive healthcare insurance and less expensive healthcare through competitive forces that lower costs.

To Repeal ObamaNet? Before discussing how fast it will take to repeal ObamaNet, some words on ObamaNet are in order. First, ObamaNet was not discussed earlier in this book because it was not a major factor in the moral outrage preceding the critical presidential election of 2016. Nevertheless, it is an exceptionally important issue to both our political freedom and our economic freedom. What is ObamaNet and why is it so vital to our political and economic freedom?

ObamaNet is essentially ObamaCare for the Internet. It's the needless, pointless and useless regulation of a private sector industry that has thrived without government aid or interference or intervention. It's the senseless regulation of an economic powerhouse for the American Economy that will likely result in considerably higher costs for consumers and businesses; markedly diminished technological investment and innovation; substantially restricted new business model creation; noticeably constrained performance and capacity (speeds and bandwidth); and strikingly reduced numbers of new apps, tools and services.

Before the Federal Communications Commission's (FCC) implementation of ObamaNet in 2015, it was debated under the name of "Net Neutrality." Bottom line, from an economic point of view, ObamaNet makes no sense whatsoever.

If that's not bad enough, however, there's another big threat from ObamaNet. ObamaNet also opens up the door to the real danger of restrictions on our freedom of speech. Why?

There are two primary reasons for concern that ObamaNet will lead to restrictions on political speech over the Internet. One deals with regulating free expression under the FCC ObamaNet regulations. The other is with the Obama administration's decision to relinquish American control of the Internet to an international consortium of countries.

The latter concern is an administration-backed, Department of Commerce decision to give away the Internet. This decision is separate from the FCC policy to implement net neutrality; but, it's closely related and highly damaging to American interests.

The Internet has operated under the Internet Corporation for Assigned Names and Numbers (ICANN), a non-profit California-based organization, with freedom. American oversight of the Internet has protected Internet freedom since its inception. Websites have never been required to hold politically correct views or to follow any repressive governments' preferences for censorship on political issues.

Giving up control of the Internet, long protected and overseen by America, to an international consortium of countries, is simply another unwise decision in the ObamaNet portfolio of Internet policies.

How fast will it take to repeal ObamaNet? The answer is that you can expect ObamaNet to be repealed by presidential and Congressional action in the first 90 days of the new conservative administration.

In addition, the newly elected conservative president will probably nominate several new FCC commissioners as the current commissioners' terms expire. This will help to assure that more conservative policies, including pro-growth economic policies that support technological and business model innovation, are developed and implemented, benefiting the American Economy in the long run.

To Repeal ObamaFood and Get Good School Lunches Again? Stories are legion of unhappy school children being fed skimpy, tasteless, and draconian meals in their schools. Certainly, our children and grandchildren deserve better than a meager third world diet.

How fast will it take to repeal ObamaFood and get good school lunches again? The answer is about seven or eight months (August 2017 – September 2017) after Inauguration Day. That's the time it will likely take for the conservative president working with Congress to introduce and pass legislation for a new school nutrition program that features food our children will enjoy eating and will still be nutritious for them from the point of view of salt, sugar, whole grain and caloric content. Implementation in school districts across America will follow. Expect good lunches to start returning to school districts across America in the Fall 2017.

To Create a Booming Economy? Of great important to the nation is a robust and booming economy. GDP growth of 3% to 5% should be the norm, not the exception.

Anticipate that both the new conservative president and Congress will pursue strong and consistent pro-growth economic policies, including pro-growth tax policies, spending policies, regulatory policies, and monetary policies. Expect both the new president and Congress to adhere to the core principles of the new Conservative Era.

Toward the goals of super-charging the American Economy and creating a new level of prosperity across America, the new president and Congress will create an empowering pro-growth tax plan, spending policies that slim down the waste and redundancy in the Federal government cost structure, and regulatory policies that thin out needless and costly bureaucratic red tape.

The president will also influence Federal Reserve monetary policy by appointments to the Federal Reserve. In the new Conservative Era, sensible rule-based monetary policies that are pro-growth will likely be followed once again.

How fast will it take to create a booming economy? The answer is about three years. The great engine of the American Economy has been stifled for years. It will take time to rev it up again. But, it will come back with a strong pro-growth president and Congress. Here's the timeline to a robust and booming economy.

In the first 90 days, the president, his economic leadership team, and the Congress agree on pro-growth tax, spending and regulatory policies. In the second 90 days, legislation is created, developed, passed by Congress, and signed into law by the president.

In those first 180 days, the Federal Reserve in parallel begins altering the course of monetary policy away from the pre-election Qualitative Easing policies toward more proven rule-based monetary policies, such as the Taylor Rule mentioned in an earlier Chapter, that help to create a stable money supply.

As the pro-growth policies kick into action and as the private sector adjusts to increased economic freedom, the economy will once again bounce back strongly and will start growing. GDP numbers will start rising significantly. GDP growth rates will probably hit the 3% to 5% levels within 3 years.

To Rebuild Our Military Strength? Threats abound to America's security and the new conservative president and Congress will tackle those national security issues as an extraordinarily high priority immediately at the start of the new administration.

I think America's top military leaders, strategists and planners under orders from the new conservative president will develop a new overall threats assessment planning document to be ready for the president within 90 days of Inauguration Day. Specifically, I expect that they will address the threats at three levels: (1) imminent threats; (2) tactical threats; and (3) strategic and long-range threats. Some responses are probably done quickly and easily, while others require new legislation and funding. Some might require long-term answers that necessitate considerable new, advanced weapons systems R&D.

The president, along with the Secretary of Defense and the Joint Chiefs of Staff, and Congress will address these threats as quickly as possible. Actual responses and timing of these responses is appropriately beyond the knowledge and scope of this book.

How fast will it take to rebuild our military strength? The answer is a comprehensive threats assessment will probably occur within the first 90 days after Inauguration Day. To fully restore our clear military strength and superiority as well as to address adequately and thoroughly all of our national security threats, I envision a three year timeframe.

To Get a Conservative Majority on the Supreme Court?
Preceding the critical presidential election of 2016, conservatives

didn't hold a decisive majority on the Supreme Court. Recent highly questionable Supreme Court decisions prove that point.

In 2017, on their respective birthdays, Supreme Court justices should be the following ages: Chief Justice Roberts – 62; Associate Justice Scalia – 81; Associate Justice Kennedy – 81; Associate Justice Thomas – 69; Associate Justice Ginsburg – 84; Associate Justice Breyer – 79; Associate Justice Alito – 67; Associate Justice Sotomayor – 63; and Associate Justice Kagan – 57.

Assuming justices might choose to retire in their 80's, the new conservative president will probably nominate four Supreme Court justices in their first term of office. Certainly, adding four new conservative Supreme Court justices will assure a decidedly conservative point of view on the Supreme Court. This will all but assure the Constitution and the Rule of Law will be upheld in Supreme Court decisions in the Conservative Era.

How fast will it take to get a conservative majority on the Supreme Court? The answer is probably within two to three years at most after Inauguration Day. It might even happen sooner, depending on when justices actually choose to retire from the Supreme Court.

Prediction #10
I predict within the new president's first term of office four new conservative justices will be appointed to the Supreme Court and approved by the Senate. It is likely that three of these four new justices will replace progressive justices currently on the court. Without question, these three new conservative justices will move the court to a more originalist interpretation of the Constitution. This will also assure a new American Constitutional Era, the Conservative Era, will begin with the critical presidential election of 2016 and the election of a new conservative president.

Part VI

Great News for America

Chapter 14

America's Future is Bright and Beautiful!

America's future is truly bright and beautiful. But, first, as a nation, we need to recognize and leave the dismal progressive legacy of failure in the "ash heap of history."[247]

It's Time to Leave the Progressive Legacy of Failure in the "Ash Heap of History"

Progressives have spent over a hundred years condemning America, the greatest nation ever to exist on the earth. Progressives have spent decades upon decades disparaging our Constitution, the greatest political document ever written in the history of civilization for guaranteeing liberty and justice for its citizens. Progressives have spent countless years distorting economic theories and realities, all with the goal of obtaining power over the people, and taking away the precious freedom of individuals.

But, worst of all, progressives have spent their energies in the pursuit of fundamentally transforming America into a progressive socialist form of government that dissipates our freedoms, usurps our resources, and controls our lives from a centralized, cold-hearted, unloving, oversized and bloated government. All the while they do these things, they feign good intentions, and pretend to be doing their bad deeds for us (rather than for the power they get over us).

Look around at the wreckage of progressive socialism during the Entitlement Era and the Anti-Constitutional Era. Our culture is in moral decline. There are rampant numbers of abortions. There are enormous numbers of broken marriages and fragmented families living in pain and poverty. There are racial and ethnic groups pitted against one another by politicians in a cynical attempt to hold voting blocs together and maintain power.

In truth, our cities are filled with racial tension, staggering crime rates, and the police restricted, immobilized, and fearful of enforcing the laws. Our political system is filled with corruption and cronyism, unresponsive to voter needs, and ignoring political promises. Our elections are filled with negative campaign ads that attack people and avoid issues. Our citizens are filled with fears about violating the progressive rules of political correctness, lest they lose their jobs or their careers.

The American Economy is battered with high and burdensome taxes, extravagant and wasteful spending, complex and convoluted regulations spanning the various economic sectors and industries. Unemployment statistics mask the true situation where over 94 million Americans are not participating in the workforce. Our GDP numbers are remarkably low and show little signs of a strong, robust recovery that Americans are used to seeing after a recession. Progressive policies have failed Americans from coast-to-coast.

Progressive foreign policy choices, military downsizing, and border decisions have left America vulnerable to strategic, tactical and terrorist threats. Other countries flaunt our perceived weaknesses and no longer look to America for moral and political leadership.

Across America, our religious freedom, political freedom, and economic freedom are all in retreat. Our Constitution and the Rule of Law have been grossly ignored and violated.

In truth and reality, America has reaped a dismal legacy of failure from progressive socialism. It's time to recognize and leave that awful legacy of progressive failure in the "ash heap of history."[248]

Americans Seek – Morality and Freedom, Peace and Prosperity

Americans – regardless of sex, sexual orientation, marital status, age, race, ethnic origin, geographical location, education, economic status, faith, religious beliefs or religion, or any other demographic factor or human quality – seek the same precise things in life.

Americans need, want, desire, and seek morality and freedom, peace and prosperity, with compassion for themselves, their families, their friends, their nation, and the world. It's part of the human psyche.

God created one, large and beautiful family of human beings. There are no true boundaries between the needs and desires of human beings. The ism's of failure should not attempt to create boundaries among people and isolate groups of human beings for the selfish purpose of obtaining and keeping power over others.

Also, the long-standing attempt by socialists to divide and conquer human beings does not make theoretical or practical sense. Dividing Americans into groups, pitting one group against another group, for the purpose of gaining political power over some groups, is fundamentally disruptive and immoral. It doesn't bring people together; it tears them apart with distrust, hatred and animosity. It's the antithesis of love.

Dividing up Americans by sexes, by sexual orientation, by age groups, by marital status, by age groups, by racial groups, by ethnic groups, by geographical locations, by educational achievements, by economic income groups (for example, the 1% vs. the others), or by other factors (for example, obese Americans, or climate change "deniers") creates tension and ignores our real needs as human beings.

In stark contrast, those who believe in the core principles of the new Conservative Era, think that all Americans truly seek to live with morality. For example, all Americans want to live in a neighborhood free from crime. Who wants to live in fear of their home being robbed? Who wants to think their teenager might get shot on the way home from school? Who wants to have their car stolen when parked at a shopping center?

Conservatives also believe that all Americans, not just certain groups of Americans, truly seek freedom in their lives. All Americans want religious freedom, political freedom, and economic freedom. Who wants to live in fear that they will be fired from a job because they mentioned their religious beliefs? Who wants to be ostracized because they talked about their political beliefs in public? Who wants to come up against so many complex regulations that they can't start a small business to improve their life and fulfill a long-held dream of running their own business?

Conservatives also believe that all Americans genuinely desire peace and prosperity in their personal lives, in America, and around the world. Who wants to experience tension and strife because you happen to be in a different progressive-defined group? Who wants America to be at war with another nation? Who wants terrorists threatening our lives right here in America? Plus, on the other hand, who doesn't want to live a better life, with a higher income, and a better standard of living?

While progressives believe they must focus on taking down some groups in order to supposedly bring up other groups, conservatives believe we are all deep down inside the same, the same human beings, with the same needs, and we should build up all Americans, not just some Americans, and certainly not at the expense of any other Americans.

Conservatives believe John F. Kennedy's words that "... a rising tide lifts all boats,"[249] and conservatives believe we should all work toward lifting that tide, for all Americans to be raised up with it.

A Record-Setting Voter Turnout

As I mentioned earlier, the critical presidential election of 2016 will likely see a record-setting voter turnout. More Americans will probably vote than in any preceding presidential election in the history of America. Literally, my forecast is for tens of millions of additional voters to participate in the election that have not previously voted. Why? Because they will be expressing their deeply held moral outrage at the direction the nation has taken in the Anti-Constitutional Era. Voters will be voting to sweep away the dismal legacy of failed progressive promises, policies and programs.

Groups that in the past were loyal to progressive politicians and supported socialists policies and programs will break away from these policies and programs and look instead to conservative core principles. Rather than maintaining their allegiances to identity group politics, they will see the futility of progressive socialism and realign their political affiliations. Groups of the past will splinter dramatically, shocking many in the establishment elite.

Expect two major voting outcomes during the critical presidential election of 2016. First, expect there to be tens of millions of new conservative voters, many of whom are Christian who seek to keep America's guarantees of true religious freedom, political freedom, and economic freedom. Second, millions of formerly loyal progressive voting bloc members will fragment from their past voting habits and will vote for morality and freedom, peace and prosperity. These voters will adopt a new political party and a new political home. They will join with other conservatives with traditional values.

A New Day and a New Conservative Era
Americans truly seek morality and freedom, peace and prosperity. They will be fooled no longer by empty promises and worn out rhetoric. They will ignore campaign TV ads and pundit arguments that inaccurately and unfairly attack a candidate's character and record.

The critical presidential election of 2016 will be the third conservative election landslide in a decade and will give a clear conservative mandate to the new president and Congress. Americans will speak with one, loud, clear voice. It's time for a big change. It's time for a new day. It's time for a new Conservative Era.

America's Future is Bright and Beautiful!
It's difficult to imagine the next 100 years in America. Truly, it will be bright and beautiful.

It will be filled with a new re-birth of spiritual and personal growth.

It will see new meaning, new knowledge, new solutions, new ideas, new technologies, new products, new services, new tools, new apps, new businesses, new jobs, new non-profits that serve humanity, new recreation, new leisure time activities, new vistas, new horizons, and new opportunities galore.

It will be characterized by enormous economic growth and prosperity, and phenomenally high standards of living for Americans and those around the world that practice morality and freedom and promote peace and prosperity. It will also see the national debt paid off from the proceeds of our prosperity.

It will foster new theological and philosophical understanding of the world because our level of prosperity can fund such endeavors. The arts and sciences will flourish and soar to new heights. Technology will stagger our minds and serve our needs in ways not thought possible today.

It will be a time when our individual lives and lifestyles will be robust and healthy, with the major diseases of today conquered by advanced medical research and development.

It will be a remarkable time to be alive.

It will be a remarkable time to be an American.

It all starts now with the historic and critical presidential election of 2016 and the dawning of the new Conservative Era.

God bless America.

Other Books by the Author

Renewing America and Its Heritage of Freedom

America's Economic War

Choosing the Good Life

About the Author

Gerard Francis Lameiro Ph.D. is an author, philosopher, economist, and engineer. He is the author of three other books and is a popular Talk Radio show guest that currently does about three hundred media interviews annually across America.

He has worked on many political campaigns in various roles, including Ronald Reagan's 1976 and 1980 presidential election campaigns. Dr. Lameiro was a member of the 1980 Presidential Electoral College and personally cast one electoral vote for Ronald Reagan as President of the United States of America.

He was the Founder and CEO of Lameiro Economics LLC, a company focused on bringing practical economic knowledge about freedom, economic growth, and prosperity to America and to the world.

He was a member of Hewlett-Packard's Strategy and Corporate Development team. He was the worldwide President of the Association of Energy Engineers (AEE) and a National Science Foundation Post-Doctoral Fellow. He was also an Assistant Professor in Colorado State University's College of Business.

Dr. Lameiro is an expert in economic growth, analytics and computer modeling.

For more information on Dr. Lameiro, please visit: GreatNewsForAmerica.com .

Notes

1 Gerard Francis Lameiro, *Renewing America and Its Heritage of Freedom: What Freedom-Loving Americans Can Do to Help* (Fort Collins, CO: Gerard Francis Lameiro, 2014), pp. 9 – 35.

2 Samuel P. Huntington, *American Politics: The Promise of Disharmony* (Cambridge, MA and London, England: The Belknap Press of Harvard University Press, 1981), p. 123.

3 Samuel P. Huntington, *American Politics: The Promise of Disharmony* (Cambridge, MA and London, England: The Belknap Press of Harvard University Press, 1981), pp. 122 – 129, pp. 167 – 169.

4 Ken Kollman, *The American Political System, Second Core Edition* (New York, NY: W. W. Norton & Company, Inc., 2014, 2013, 2012), pp. 424 – 435.

5 Noble E. Cunningham Jr., "Election of 1800," *History of American Presidential Elections 1789 – 2008, Fourth Edition, Volume I: 1789 – 1868,* Gil Troy, Arthur M. Schlesinger Jr. and Fred L. Israel, Editors (New York, NY: Facts On File, Inc., An Imprint of Infobase Learning, 2012), pp. 49 – 78.

6 Noble E. Cunningham Jr., "Election of 1800," *History of American Presidential Elections 1789 – 2008, Fourth Edition, Volume I: 1789 – 1868,* Gil Troy, Arthur M. Schlesinger Jr. and Fred L. Israel, Editors (New York, NY: Facts On File, Inc., An Imprint of Infobase Learning, 2012), pp. 49 – 78.

7 Samuel P. Huntington, *American Politics: The Promise of Disharmony* (Cambridge, MA and London, England: The Belknap Press of Harvard University Press, 1981), p. 86.

8 Robert H. Bork, *The Tempting of America: The Political Seduction of the Law* (New York, NY: Touchstone, Simon & Schuster, 1990), pp. 20 – 28.

9 Robert H. Bork, *The Tempting of America: The Political Seduction of the Law* (New York, NY: Touchstone, Simon & Schuster, 1990), p. 24.

10 While some political historians might prefer to delimit the end of the Jacksonian Era in the early 1850s, I prefer to run it out to 1860 because we are looking at long range political time periods and not simply single point elections. For me, the Jacksonian Era ranges from the end of the Constitutional Era to the critical election of 1860.

11 Robert V. Remini, *Andrew Jackson: Volume Two: The Course of American Freedom, 1822 – 1832* (Baltimore, MD: The Johns Hopkins University Press, 1981), pp. 12 – 38.

12 Robert V. Remini, *Andrew Jackson: Volume Two: The Course of American Freedom, 1822 – 1832* (Baltimore, MD: The Johns Hopkins University Press, 1981), pp. 30 – 31.

13 Robert V. Remini, "Election of 1828," *History of American Presidential Elections 1789 – 2008, Fourth Edition, Volume I: 1789 – 1868,* Gil Troy, Arthur M. Schlesinger Jr. and Fred L. Israel, Editors (New York, NY: Facts On File, Inc., An Imprint of Infobase Learning, 2012), pp. 202 – 225.

14 James F. Hopkins, "Election of 1824," *History of American Presidential Elections 1789 – 2008, Fourth Edition, Volume I: 1789 – 1868,* Gil Troy, Arthur M. Schlesinger Jr. and Fred L. Israel, Editors (New York, NY: Facts On File, Inc., An Imprint of Infobase Learning, 2012), p. 170.

15 Robert V. Remini, "Election of 1828," *History of American Presidential Elections 1789 – 2008, Fourth Edition, Volume I: 1789 – 1868,* Gil Troy, Arthur M. Schlesinger Jr. and Fred L. Israel, Editors (New York, NY: Facts On File, Inc., An Imprint of Infobase Learning, 2012), pp. 202 – 225.

16 Robert V. Remini, "Election of 1828," *History of American Presidential Elections 1789 – 2008, Fourth Edition, Volume I: 1789 – 1868,* Gil Troy, Arthur M. Schlesinger Jr. and Fred L. Israel, Editors (New York, NY: Facts On File, Inc., An Imprint of Infobase Learning, 2012), pp. 202 – 225.

17 Robert V. Remini, "Election of 1828," *History of American Presidential Elections 1789 – 2008, Fourth Edition, Volume I: 1789 – 1868,* Gil Troy, Arthur M. Schlesinger Jr. and Fred L. Israel, Editors (New York, NY: Facts On File, Inc., An Imprint of Infobase Learning, 2012), pp. 202 – 225.

18 Joel H. Silbey, "Election of 1836," *History of American Presidential Elections 1789 – 2008, Fourth Edition, Volume I: 1789 – 1868,* Gil Troy, Arthur M. Schlesinger Jr. and Fred L. Israel, Editors (New York, NY: Facts On File, Inc., An Imprint of Infobase Learning, 2012), p. 254.

19 Robert V. Remini, "Election of 1828," *History of American Presidential Elections 1789 – 2008, Fourth Edition, Volume I: 1789 – 1868,* Gil Troy, Arthur M. Schlesinger Jr. and Fred L. Israel, Editors (New York, NY: Facts On File, Inc., An Imprint of Infobase Learning, 2012), pp. 202 – 225.

[20] Joel H. Silbey, "American Political Parties: History, Voters, Critical Elections, and Party Systems," *The Oxford Handbook of American Political Parties and Interest Groups,* L. Sandy Maisel and Jeffrey M. Berry, Editors (New York, NY: Oxford University Press Inc., 2010), pp. 97 – 107.

[21] Robert V. Remini, *Andrew Jackson* (New York, NY: HarperCollins Publishers, Reprinted by arrangement with Twayne Publishers, Inc., Copyright © 1966 by Twayne Publishers, Inc., Maps copyright © 1999 by Jeffrey L. Ward), p. 118.

[22] Robert V. Remini, *Andrew Jackson* (New York, NY: HarperCollins Publishers, Reprinted by arrangement with Twayne Publishers, Inc., Copyright © 1966 by Twayne Publishers, Inc., Maps copyright © 1999 by Jeffrey L. Ward), p. 118.

[23] Joel H. Silbey, "American Political Parties: History, Voters, Critical Elections, and Party Systems," *The Oxford Handbook of American Political Parties and Interest Groups,* L. Sandy Maisel and Jeffrey M. Berry, Editors (New York, NY: Oxford University Press Inc., 2010), pp. 97 – 107.

[24] William Nisbet Chambers, "Election of 1840," *History of American Presidential Elections 1789 – 2008, Fourth Edition, Volume I: 1789 – 1868,* Gil Troy, Arthur M. Schlesinger Jr. and Fred L. Israel, Editors (New York, NY: Facts On File, Inc., An Imprint of Infobase Learning, 2012), p. 278.

[25] Holman Hamilton, "Election of 1848," *History of American Presidential Elections 1789 – 2008, Fourth Edition, Volume I: 1789 – 1868,* Gil Troy, Arthur M. Schlesinger Jr. and Fred L. Israel, Editors (New York, NY: Facts On File, Inc., An Imprint of Infobase Learning, 2012), p. 373.

[26] Joel H. Silbey, "American Political Parties: History, Voters, Critical Elections, and Party Systems," *The Oxford Handbook of American Political Parties and Interest Groups,* L. Sandy Maisel and Jeffrey M. Berry, Editors (New York, NY: Oxford University Press Inc., 2010), pp. 97 – 107.

[27] Elting Morison, "Election of 1860," *History of American Presidential Elections 1789 – 2008, Fourth Edition, Volume I: 1789 – 1868,* Gil Troy, Arthur M. Schlesinger Jr. and Fred L. Israel, Editors (New York, NY: Facts On File, Inc., An Imprint of Infobase Learning, 2012), p. 465.

[28] Elting Morison, "Election of 1860," *History of American Presidential Elections 1789 – 2008, Fourth Edition, Volume I: 1789 – 1868,* Gil Troy, Arthur M. Schlesinger Jr. and Fred L. Israel,

Editors (New York, NY: Facts On File, Inc., An Imprint of Infobase Learning, 2012), pp. 465 – 491.

29 Robert H. Bork, *The Tempting of America: The Political Seduction of the Law* (New York, NY: Touchstone, Simon & Schuster, 1990), pp. 28 – 34.

30 Robert H. Bork, *The Tempting of America: The Political Seduction of the Law* (New York, NY: Touchstone, Simon & Schuster, 1990), pp. 28 – 34.

31 Robert H. Bork, *The Tempting of America: The Political Seduction of the Law* (New York, NY: Touchstone, Simon & Schuster, 1990), pp. 28 – 34.

32 Robert H. Bork, *The Tempting of America: The Political Seduction of the Law* (New York, NY: Touchstone, Simon & Schuster, 1990), pp. 28 – 34.

33 Robert H. Bork, *The Tempting of America: The Political Seduction of the Law* (New York, NY: Touchstone, Simon & Schuster, 1990), pp. 28 – 34.

34 Steven J. Rosenstone, Roy L. Behr and Edward H. Lazarus, *Third Parties in America: Citizens Response to Major Party Failure, Second Edition, Revised and Expanded* (Princeton, NJ: Princeton University Press, 1984), pp. 56 – 59.

35 Steven J. Rosenstone, Roy L. Behr and Edward H. Lazarus, *Third Parties in America: Citizens Response to Major Party Failure, Second Edition, Revised and Expanded* (Princeton, NJ: Princeton University Press, 1984), pp. 48 – 60.

36 Robert H. Bork, *The Tempting of America: The Political Seduction of the Law* (New York, NY: Touchstone, Simon & Schuster, 1990), pp. 28 – 34, pp. 129 – 132.

37 Gilbert C. Fite, "Election of 1896," *History of American Presidential Elections 1789 – 2008, Fourth Edition, Volume II: 1872 – 1940,* Gil Troy, Arthur M. Schlesinger Jr. and Fred L. Israel, Editors (New York, NY: Facts On File, Inc., An Imprint of Infobase Learning, 2012), pp. 740 – 774.

38 Gilbert C. Fite, "Election of 1896," *History of American Presidential Elections 1789 – 2008, Fourth Edition, Volume II: 1872 – 1940,* Gil Troy, Arthur M. Schlesinger Jr. and Fred L. Israel, Editors (New York, NY: Facts On File, Inc., An Imprint of Infobase Learning, 2012), pp. 740 – 774.

39 Gilbert C. Fite, "Election of 1896," *History of American Presidential Elections 1789 – 2008, Fourth Edition, Volume II: 1872 – 1940,* Gil Troy, Arthur M. Schlesinger Jr. and Fred L. Israel,

Editors (New York, NY: Facts On File, Inc., An Imprint of Infobase Learning, 2012), pp. 740 – 774.

[40] Gilbert C. Fite, "Election of 1896," *History of American Presidential Elections 1789 – 2008, Fourth Edition, Volume II: 1872 – 1940,* Gil Troy, Arthur M. Schlesinger Jr. and Fred L. Israel, Editors (New York, NY: Facts On File, Inc., An Imprint of Infobase Learning, 2012), pp. 740 – 774.

[41] Gilbert C. Fite, "Election of 1896," *History of American Presidential Elections 1789 – 2008, Fourth Edition, Volume II: 1872 – 1940,* Gil Troy, Arthur M. Schlesinger Jr. and Fred L. Israel, Editors (New York, NY: Facts On File, Inc., An Imprint of Infobase Learning, 2012), pp. 746 – 747.

[42] Joel H. Silbey, "American Political Parties: History, Voters, Critical Elections, and Party Systems," *The Oxford Handbook of American Political Parties and Interest Groups,* L. Sandy Maisel and Jeffrey M. Berry, Editors (New York, NY: Oxford University Press Inc., 2010), pp. 112 – 115.

[43] George E. Mowry, "Election of 1912," *History of American Presidential Elections 1789 – 2008, Fourth Edition, Volume II: 1872 – 1940,* Gil Troy, Arthur M. Schlesinger Jr. and Fred L. Israel, Editors (New York, NY: Facts On File, Inc., An Imprint of Infobase Learning, 2012), pp. 877 – 907.

[44] Sidney M. Milkis, "Introduction: Progressivism, Then and Now," *Progressivism and the New Democracy,* Sidney M. Milkis and Jerome M. Mileur, Editors (Amherst, MA: The University of Massachusetts Press, 1999), pp. 1 – 39.

[45] Woodrow Wilson, *The New Freedom: A Call for the Emancipation of the Generous Energies of a People,* Originally Published by Doubleday, Page & Company in 1913, Gray Rabbit Publications edition (Brooklyn, NY: Gray Rabbit Publications, 2011).

[46] Sidney M. Milkis, "Introduction: Progressivism, Then and Now," *Progressivism and the New Democracy,* Sidney M. Milkis and Jerome M. Mileur, Editors (Amherst, MA: The University of Massachusetts Press, 1999), pp. 1 – 39.

[47] George E. Mowry, "Election of 1912," *History of American Presidential Elections 1789 – 2008, Fourth Edition, Volume II: 1872 – 1940,* Gil Troy, Arthur M. Schlesinger Jr. and Fred L. Israel, Editors (New York, NY: Facts On File, Inc., An Imprint of Infobase Learning, 2012), pp. 877 – 907.

[48] Sidney M. Milkis, "Introduction: Progressivism, Then and Now," *Progressivism and the New Democracy,* Sidney M. Milkis and

Jerome M. Mileur, Editors (Amherst, MA: The University of Massachusetts Press, 1999), pp. 1 – 39.

49 Sidney M. Milkis, "Introduction: Progressivism, Then and Now," *Progressivism and the New Democracy,* Sidney M. Milkis and Jerome M. Mileur, Editors (Amherst, MA: The University of Massachusetts Press, 1999), pp. 1 – 39.

50 Gerald C. Wright, "State Parties Research: The Quest for Strong, Competitive State Parties," *The Oxford Handbook of American Political Parties and Interest Groups,* L. Sandy Maisel and Jeffrey M. Berry, Editors (New York, NY: Oxford University Press Inc., 2010), pp. 403 – 422.

51 Sidney M. Milkis, "Introduction: Progressivism, Then and Now," *Progressivism and the New Democracy,* Sidney M. Milkis and Jerome M. Mileur, Editors (Amherst, MA: The University of Massachusetts Press, 1999), pp. 1 – 39.

52 R. Hal Williams, *Realigning America: McKinley, Bryan, and the Remarkable Election of 1896* (Lawrence, KS: University Press of Kansas, 2010), pp. 137 – 138.

53 R. Hal Williams, *Realigning America: McKinley, Bryan, and the Remarkable Election of 1896* (Lawrence, KS: University Press of Kansas, 2010), pp. 137 – 138.

54 Kevin Phillips, *William McKinley,* The American Presidents, Arthur M. Schlesinger, Jr., General Editor (New York, NY: Times Books, Henry Holt and Company, LLC, 2003), p. 67.

55 Kevin Phillips, *William McKinley,* The American Presidents, Arthur M. Schlesinger, Jr., General Editor (New York, NY: Times Books, Henry Holt and Company, LLC, 2003), pp. 77 – 78.

56Kevin Phillips, *William McKinley,* The American Presidents, Arthur M. Schlesinger, Jr., General Editor (New York, NY: Times Books, Henry Holt and Company, LLC, 2003), pp. 77 – 78.

57 Jim Powell, *FDR's Folly: How Roosevelt and His New Deal Prolonged the Great Depression* (New York, NY: Three Rivers Press, 2003), pp. 27 – 37.

58 George E. Mowry, "Election of 1912," *History of American Presidential Elections 1789 – 2008, Fourth Edition, Volume II: 1872 – 1940,* Gil Troy, Arthur M. Schlesinger Jr. and Fred L. Israel, Editors (New York, NY: Facts On File, Inc., An Imprint of Infobase Learning, 2012), pp. 877 – 907.

59 Burton Folsom, Jr., *New Deal or Raw Deal? How FDR's Economic Legacy has Damaged America* (New York, NY: Threshold Editions, A Division of Simon & Schuster, Inc., 2008), pp. 30 – 42.

[60] Milton Friedman and Anna Jacobson Schwartz, *The Great Contraction 1929 – 1933: With a New Preface by Anna Jacobson Schwartz and New Introduction by Peter L. Bernstein* (Princeton, NJ: Princeton University Press, 2008 for "New Preface" and "Introduction: The Great Contraction, Seen from the Perspective of 2007." Also, "The Great Contraction, 1929 – 1933," National Bureau of Economic Research, 1963, 1965).

[61] Frank Freidel, "Election of 1932," *History of American Presidential Elections 1789 – 2008, Fourth Edition, Volume II: 1872 – 1940,* Gil Troy, Arthur M. Schlesinger Jr. and Fred L. Israel, Editors (New York, NY: Facts On File, Inc., An Imprint of Infobase Learning, 2012), pp. 1025 – 1056.

[62] Frank Freidel, "Election of 1932," *History of American Presidential Elections 1789 – 2008, Fourth Edition, Volume II: 1872 – 1940,* Gil Troy, Arthur M. Schlesinger Jr. and Fred L. Israel, Editors (New York, NY: Facts On File, Inc., An Imprint of Infobase Learning, 2012), pp. 1025 – 1056.

[63] Robert H. Bork, *The Tempting of America: The Political Seduction of the Law* (New York, NY: Touchstone, Simon & Schuster, 1990), pp. 15 – 53.

[64] Robert H. Bork, *The Tempting of America: The Political Seduction of the Law* (New York, NY: Touchstone, Simon & Schuster, 1990), pp. 51 – 53.

[65] Robert H. Bork, *The Tempting of America: The Political Seduction of the Law* (New York, NY: Touchstone, Simon & Schuster, 1990), pp. 51 – 56.

[66] Mike Lee, *Our Lost Constitution: The Willful Subversion of America's Founding Document* (New York, NY: Sentinel, Penguin Group, Penguin Group (USA) LLC, 2015), pp. 142 – 149.

[67] Mike Lee, *Our Lost Constitution: The Willful Subversion of America's Founding Document* (New York, NY: Sentinel, Penguin Group, Penguin Group (USA) LLC, 2015), pp. 142 – 149.

[68] Mike Lee, *Our Lost Constitution: The Willful Subversion of America's Founding Document* (New York, NY: Sentinel, Penguin Group, Penguin Group (USA) LLC, 2015), pp. 142 – 149.

[69] Robert H. Bork, *The Tempting of America: The Political Seduction of the Law* (New York, NY: Touchstone, Simon & Schuster, 1990), pp. 54 – 56.

[70] Robert H. Bork, *The Tempting of America: The Political Seduction of the Law* (New York, NY: Touchstone, Simon & Schuster, 1990), pp. 69 – 100.

[71] Robert H. Bork, *The Tempting of America: The Political Seduction of the Law* (New York, NY: Touchstone, Simon & Schuster, 1990), pp. 69 – 100.

[72] Ronald Reagan, "A Time for Choosing," Nationwide Televised Address for Barry Goldwater Presidential Campaign, October 27, 1964, *The Greatest Speeches of Ronald Reagan: Introduction by Michael Reagan, 2nd Edition* (West Palm Beach, FL: NewsMax.com, Inc., 2001, "With introduction by Michael Reagan," NewsMax.com, 2002), pp. 1 – 4.

[73] John Bartlow Martin, "Election of 1964," *History of American Presidential Elections 1789 – 2008, Fourth Edition, Volume III: 1944 – 2008,* Gil Troy, Arthur M. Schlesinger Jr. and Fred L. Israel, Editors (New York, NY: Facts On File, Inc., An Imprint of Infobase Learning, 2012), pp. 1286 – 1316.

[74] John Bartlow Martin, "Election of 1964," *History of American Presidential Elections 1789 – 2008, Fourth Edition, Volume III: 1944 – 2008,* Gil Troy, Arthur M. Schlesinger Jr. and Fred L. Israel, Editors (New York, NY: Facts On File, Inc., An Imprint of Infobase Learning, 2012), pp. 1286 – 1316.

[75] John Bartlow Martin, "Election of 1964," *History of American Presidential Elections 1789 – 2008, Fourth Edition, Volume III: 1944 – 2008,* Gil Troy, Arthur M. Schlesinger Jr. and Fred L. Israel, Editors (New York, NY: Facts On File, Inc., An Imprint of Infobase Learning, 2012), pp. 1286 – 1316.

[76] Robert H. Bork, *The Tempting of America: The Political Seduction of the Law* (New York, NY: Touchstone, Simon & Schuster, 1990), pp. 95 – 100.

[77] Robert H. Bork, *The Tempting of America: The Political Seduction of the Law* (New York, NY: Touchstone, Simon & Schuster, 1990), pp. 95 – 100.

[78] Robert H. Bork, *The Tempting of America: The Political Seduction of the Law* (New York, NY: Touchstone, Simon & Schuster, 1990), pp. 28 – 34 and pp. 95 – 100.

[79] Robert H. Bork, *The Tempting of America: The Political Seduction of the Law* (New York, NY: Touchstone, Simon & Schuster, 1990), pp. 95 – 100 and pp. 110 – 126.

[80] Robert H. Bork, *Coercing Virtue: The Worldwide Rule of Judges* (Washington, DC: The AEI Press, Publisher for the American Enterprise Institute, 2003), pp. 78 – 79.

[81] James T. Patterson, *The Eve of Destruction: How 1965 Transformed America* (New York, NY: Basic Books, A Member of

the Perseus Books Group, 2012), p. xvi.

[82] Stephen M. Krason, "1965: The Dawn of Our Current Age," June 5, 2015, *Crisis Magazine*, http://www.crisismagazine.com/2015/1965-the-dawn-of-our-current-age .

[83] Stephen M. Krason, "1965: The Dawn of Our Current Age," June 5, 2015, *Crisis Magazine*, http://www.crisismagazine.com/2015/1965-the-dawn-of-our-current-age .

[84] Jules Witcover, "Election of 1980," *History of American Presidential Elections 1789 – 2008, Fourth Edition, Volume III: 1944 – 2008,* Gil Troy, Arthur M. Schlesinger Jr. and Fred L. Israel, Editors (New York, NY: Facts On File, Inc., An Imprint of Infobase Learning, 2012), pp. 1416 – 1445.

[85] Andrew E. Busch, *Reagan's Victory: The Presidential Election of 1980 and the Rise of the Right* (Lawrence, KS: University Press of Kansas, 2005), p. 11.

[86] Andrew E. Busch, *Reagan's Victory: The Presidential Election of 1980 and the Rise of the Right* (Lawrence, KS: University Press of Kansas, 2005), pp. 5 – 6.

[87] Andrew E. Busch, *Reagan's Victory: The Presidential Election of 1980 and the Rise of the Right* (Lawrence, KS: University Press of Kansas, 2005), pp. 1 – 11.

[88] Arthur B. Laffer, Stephen Moore, and Peter J. Tanous, *The End of Prosperity: How Higher Taxes Will Doom the Economy – If We Let It Happen* (New York, NY: Threshold Editions, A Division of Simon & Schuster, Inc., 2008), pp. 82 – 83.

[89] Arthur B. Laffer, Stephen Moore, and Peter J. Tanous, *The End of Prosperity: How Higher Taxes Will Doom the Economy – If We Let It Happen* (New York, NY: Threshold Editions, A Division of Simon & Schuster, Inc., 2008), p. 13.

[90] Andrew E. Busch, *Reagan's Victory: The Presidential Election of 1980 and the Rise of the Right* (Lawrence, KS: University Press of Kansas, 2005), pp. 1 – 28.

[91] Andrew E. Busch, *Reagan's Victory: The Presidential Election of 1980 and the Rise of the Right* (Lawrence, KS: University Press of Kansas, 2005), pp. 1 – 28.

[92] Andrew E. Busch, *Reagan's Victory: The Presidential Election of 1980 and the Rise of the Right* (Lawrence, KS: University Press of Kansas, 2005), pp. 1 – 28.

[93] Andrew E. Busch, *Reagan's Victory: The Presidential Election of*

1980 and the Rise of the Right (Lawrence, KS: University Press of Kansas, 2005), p. 11.

[94] *King v. Burwell* 576 U. S. ___ (2015).

[95] *King v. Burwell* 576 U. S. ___ (2015).

[96] *Obergefell v. Hodges* 576 U. S. ___ (2015).

[97] Courtney Coren, "Justice Samuel Alito: Gay Marriage Ruling Could Extend to Abolishing Min. Wage," Newsmax Media, Inc., July 21, 2015, http://www.newsmax.com/Newsfront/samuel-alito-supreme-court-same-sex-marriage-ruling/2015/07/21/id/658271/ .

[98] Kristina Peterson, "Congressional Republicans Signal Deep Resistance to Iran Nuclear Deal," *The Wall Street Journal,* July 14, 2015, http://www.wsj.com/articles/iran-deal-faces-u-s-lawmakers-scrutiny-1436868209 .

[99] "Obama's U. N. First Gambit," *The Wall Street Journal,* July 20, 2015, http://www.wsj.com/articles/obamas-u-n-first-gambit-1437435308 .

[100] Christina Sandefur, "ACA Lawlessness Plaques the States," Spring 2015, *Regulation,* pp. 18 – 21, http://object.cato.org/sites/cato.org/files/serials/files/regulation/2015/3/regulation-v38n1-2.pdf .

[101] Juliet Eilperin and Zachary A. Goldfarb, "IRS officials in Washington were involved in targeting of conservative groups," *The Washington Post,* May 13, 2013, http://www.washingtonpost.com/...rted-irs-targeting-of-conservative-groups/2013/05/13/a0185644-bbdf-11e2-97d4-a479289a31f9_story.html .

[102] John Hinderaker, "Senate Hearing Highlights Problem of Illegal Immigrant Crime," *Powerline Blog,* July 21, 2015, http://www.powerlineblog.com/archives/2015/07/senate-hearing-highlights-problem-of-illegal-immigrant-crime.php .

[103] Abraham Lincoln, *Abraham Lincoln: Speeches and Writings 1859 – 1865: Speeches, Letters, and Miscellaneous Writings, Presidential Messages and Proclamations* (New York, NY: The Library of America, Literary Classics of the United States, Inc., 1989), p. 536.

[104] Samuel P. Huntington, *American Politics: The Promise of Disharmony* (Cambridge, MA and London, England: The Belknap Press of Harvard University Press, 1981), p. 99 – 102.

[105] Samuel P. Huntington, *American Politics: The Promise of Disharmony* (Cambridge, MA and London, England: The Belknap Press of Harvard University Press, 1981), p. 99 – 102.

106 Samuel P. Huntington, *American Politics: The Promise of Disharmony* (Cambridge, MA and London, England: The Belknap Press of Harvard University Press, 1981), p. 99 – 102.

107 Theodore C. Sorensen, "Election of 1960," *History of American Presidential Elections 1789 – 2008, Fourth Edition, Volume III: 1944 – 2008,* Gil Troy, Arthur M. Schlesinger Jr. and Fred L. Israel, Editors (New York, NY: Facts On File, Inc., An Imprint of Infobase Learning, 2012), pp. 1261 – 1285.

108 John Bartlow Martin, "Election of 1964," *History of American Presidential Elections 1789 – 2008, Fourth Edition, Volume III: 1944 – 2008,* Gil Troy, Arthur M. Schlesinger Jr. and Fred L. Israel, Editors (New York, NY: Facts On File, Inc., An Imprint of Infobase Learning, 2012), pp. 1286 – 1316.

109 F. A. Hayek, *The Road to Serfdom: A Classic Warning against the Dangers to Freedom Inherent in Social Planning* (Chicago, IL: The University of Chicago Press, 1944, renewed 1972), pp. 153 – 166.

110 If the reader wants to explore these particular topics in greater depth than space permits here, please read my two books: *Renewing America and Its Heritage of Freedom* for more on truth, morality and freedom; and *America's Economic War* for more on the philosophical battle between capitalism and socialism.

111 John R. Lott, Jr., *More Guns, Less Crime: Understanding Crime and Gun-Control Laws, Third Edition* (Chicago, IL: The University of Chicago Press, 1998, 2000, 2010).

112 John R. Lott, Jr., *More Guns, Less Crime: Understanding Crime and Gun-Control Laws, Third Edition* (Chicago, IL: The University of Chicago Press, 1998, 2000, 2010).

113 Awr Hawkins, "Obama's Secretive Gun Ban for Social Security Beneficiaries," Breitbart.com, July, 18, 2015, http://www.breitbart.com/big-government/2015/07/18/obamas-secretive-gun-ban-for-social-security-beneficiaries/ .

114 John R. Lott, Jr., *More Guns, Less Crime: Understanding Crime and Gun-Control Laws, Third Edition* (Chicago, IL: The University of Chicago Press, 1998, 2000, 2010).

115 James Madison, "The Federalist XLVII," New York, February 1, 1788, *The Federalist* (Washington, DC: Regnery Publishing, Inc., 1998), pp. 373 – 374.

116 Hans von Spakovsky, "Government Persecution of Wisconsin Conservatives Finally Comes to an End," *The Daily Signal,* dailysignal.com, July 17, 2015,

http://dailysignal.com/2015/07/17/government-persecution-of-wisconsin-conservatives-finally-comes-to-an-end/ .

117 Hans von Spakovsky, "Government Persecution of Wisconsin Conservatives Finally Comes to an End," *The Daily Signal,* dailysignal.com, July 17, 2015, http://dailysignal.com/2015/07/17/government-persecution-of-wisconsin-conservatives-finally-comes-to-an-end/ .

118 Hans von Spakovsky, "Government Persecution of Wisconsin Conservatives Finally Comes to an End," *The Daily Signal,* dailysignal.com, July 17, 2015, http://dailysignal.com/2015/07/17/government-persecution-of-wisconsin-conservatives-finally-comes-to-an-end/ .

119 John Fund and Hans von Spakovsky, *Obama's Enforcer: Eric Holder's Justice Department* (New York, NY: Broadside Books, HarperCollins Publishers, 2014).

120 Gerard Francis Lameiro, *Renewing America and Its Heritage of Freedom: What Freedom-Loving Americans Can Do to Help* (Fort Collins, CO: Gerard Francis Lameiro, 2014), pp. 224 – 229.

121 Patrick Howley, "EMAIL: Missouri Democratic Governor ORDERED National Guard to Stand Down During Ferguson Riots," *The Daily Caller,* dailycaller.com, January 22, 2015, http://dailycaller.com/2015/01/22/email-missouri-democratic-governor-ordered-national-guard-to-stand-down-during-ferguson-riots/ .

122 Jason L. Riley, "The Lawbreakers of Baltimore – and Ferguson," *The Wall Street Journal,* wsj.com, April 28, 2015, http://www.wsj.com/articles/the-lawbreakers-of-baltimoreand-ferguson-1430263032 .

123 William McGurn, "Baltimore Is Not About Race," *The Wall Street Journal,* wsj.com, May 4, 2015, http://www.wsj.com/articles/baltimore-is-not-about-race-1430781505 .

124 Heather Mac Donald, "The New Nationwide Crime Wave," *The Wall Street Journal,* wsj.com, May 29, 2015, http://www.wsj.com/articles/the-new-nationwide-crime-wave-1432938425 .

125 Heather Mac Donald, "The New Nationwide Crime Wave," *The Wall Street Journal,* wsj.com, May 29, 2015, http://www.wsj.com/articles/the-new-nationwide-crime-wave-1432938425 .

126 Heather Mac Donald, "The New Nationwide Crime Wave," *The*

Wall Street Journal, wsj.com, May 29, 2015, http://www.wsj.com/articles/the-new-nationwide-crime-wave-1432938425 .

127 Jason L. Riley, "The Lawbreakers of Baltimore – and Ferguson," *The Wall Street Journal,* wsj.com, April 28, 2015, http://www.wsj.com/articles/the-lawbreakers-of-baltimoreand-ferguson-1430263032 .

128 William McGurn, "Baltimore Is Not About Race," *The Wall Street Journal,* wsj.com, May 4, 2015, http://www.wsj.com/articles/baltimore-is-not-about-race-1430781505 .

129 Pam Key, "AZ Sheriff Paul Babeu: Drug Cartels With AK-47s Control American Soil 30 Miles from Phoenix," Breitbart.com, August 20, 2015, http://www.breitbart.com/video/2015/08/20/az-sheriff-paul-babeu-drug-cartels-with-ak-47s-control-american-soil-30-miles-from-phoenix/ .

130 FoxNews.com, "Purported ISIS warning claims terror cells in place in 15 states," FoxNews.com, May 6, 2015, http://www.foxnews.com/us/2015/05/06/purported-isis-warning-claims-terror-cells-in-place-in-15-states/ .

131 IBD Editorial, "A New Border Surge Opens Us To Surge Of Epidemics," *Investor's Business Daily,* September 26, 2014, http://news.investors.com/ibd-editorials/092614-719288-a-new-border-surge-opens-us-to-a-new-wave-of-diseases.htm .

132 Natalie Johnson, "California to Subsidize Health Care for Illegal Immigrant Children," ," *The Daily Signal,* dailysignal.com, June 19, 2015, http://dailysignal.com//2015/06/19/california-to-subsidize-healthcare-for-illegal-immigrant-children/ .

133 David Inserra, "Terrorist Plot 72: Congress Needs to Address Rising Islamist Terrorism at Home," Issue Brief #4438 on Terrorism, *The Heritage Foundation,* July 22, 2015, http://www.heritage.org/research/reports/2015/07/terrorist-plot-72-congress-needs-to-address-rising-islamist-terrorism-at-home .

134 David Inserra, "Terrorist Plot 72: Congress Needs to Address Rising Islamist Terrorism at Home," Issue Brief #4438 on Terrorism, *The Heritage Foundation,* July 22, 2015, http://www.heritage.org/research/reports/2015/07/terrorist-plot-72-congress-needs-to-address-rising-islamist-terrorism-at-home .

135 Courtney Coren, "IG Report: TSA Approved 73 Airport Employees Flagged for Terrorism," Newsmax Media, Inc., June 8, 2015, http://www.newsmax.com/Newsfront/tsa-airport-security-

terrorism/2015/06/08/id/649416/ .

136 Kristi Eaton, Corinne Lestch and Corky Siemaszko, "Oklahoma man beheads woman, stabs 2nd victim during workplace fight day after being fired from job," *New York Daily News,* September 26, 2014, http://www.nydailynews.com/news/crime/okla-man-beheads-woman-workplace-fight-report-article-1.1953778 .

137 Richard Perez-Pena and Michael S. Schmidt, "Woman Is Beheaded in Attack at Oklahoma Food Plant," *The New York Times,* September 26, 2014, http://www.nytimes.com/2014/09/27/us/oklahoma-man-is-said-to-behead-co-worker.html?_r=0 .

138 FoxNews.com, "Sailor shot in Tenn. terror attack dies; gunman reportedly failed drug test at nuclear plant," FoxNews.com, July 19, 2015, http://www.foxnews.com/us/2015/07/19/sailor-in-chattanooga-shooting-has-died-death-toll-now-5/ .

139 Fox News Insider, The Official Blog of Fox News Channel, "Chattanooga Shooter Identified as Muhammad Youssef Abdulazeez," FoxNews.com, July 16, 2015, http://insider.foxnews.com/2015/07/16/chattanooga-tennessee-shooter-identified-muhammad-youssef-abdulazeez .

140 Greg Botelho and Rene Marsh, "FAA: 12 commercial flights over New Jersey report lasers," Cable News Network, Turner Broadcasting System, Inc., August 15, 2015, http://www.cnn.com/2015/07/16/us/lasers-flights-new-jersey/ .

141 Greg Botelho and Rene Marsh, "FAA: 12 commercial flights over New Jersey report lasers," Cable News Network, Turner Broadcasting System, Inc., August 15, 2015, http://www.cnn.com/2015/07/16/us/lasers-flights-new-jersey/ .

142 Patrick Tucker, "Every Country Will Have Armed Drones Within 10 Years," Defense One, National Journal Group, Inc., May 6, 2014, http://www.defenseone.com/technology/2014/05/every-country-will-have-armed-drones-within-ten-years/83878/ .

143 ABC News via Good Morning America, "FAA Probing Reports of Drones, Green Lasers Over New York," ABC News Internet Ventures, May 29, 2015, http://abcnews.go.com/US/green-lasers-illuminate-flights-york/story?id=31385570 .

144 Frederick Kagan, "Why They're Cheering in Tehran," *The Wall Street Journal,* July 14, 2015, http://www.wsj.com/articles/why-theyre-cheering-in-tehran-1436916912 .

145 Frederick Kagan, "Why They're Cheering in Tehran," *The Wall Street Journal,* July 14, 2015, http://www.wsj.com/articles/why-

theyre-cheering-in-tehran-1436916912 .

146 Security Council, "Security Council, Adopting Resolution 2231 (2015), Endorses Joint Comprehensive Agreement on Iran's Nuclear Programme," Security Council Meetings Coverage, 7488th Meeting (AM), The United Nations, July 20, 2015, http://www.un.org/press/en/2015/sc11974.doc.htm .

147 The Heritage Foundation, "DeMint Statement on Iran Nuclear Deal," *The Heritage Foundation,* July 14, 2015, http://www.heritage.org/research/reports/2015/07/demint-statement-on-iran-nuclear-deal?ac=1 .

148 Edwin J. Feulner, "Why the Iran deal makes war more likely," *The Heritage Foundation,* August 18, 2015, http://www.heritage.org/research/commentary/2015/8/why-the-iran-deal-makes-war-more-likely .

149 U. S. Department of State Diplomacy in Action, "State Sponsors of Terrorism," U. S. Department of State, www.state.gov on August 29, 2015, http://www.state.gov/j/ct/list/c14151.htm .

150 Jennifer Rubin, Right Turn Blog, "The latest Iran revelation is utterly humiliating," *The Washington Post,* August 19, 2015, https://www.washingtonpost.com/blogs/right-turn/wp/2015/08/19/the-latest-iran-revelation-is-utterly-humiliating/ .

151 Bill Gertz, "Nuclear Deal Silent on Iran's Parchin Military Plant, Bushehr," *The Washington Free Beacon,* July 14, 2015, http://freebeacon.com/national-security/nuclear-deal-silent-on-irans-parchin-military-plant-bushehr/ .

152 William Tobey, "The Iranian Nuclear-Inspection Charade," *The Wall Street Journal,* July 15, 2015, http://www.wsj.com/articles/the-iranian-nuclear-inspection-charade-1437001048 .

153 Kim R. Holmes, "Why the Iran ideal increases the risk of war," *The Heritage Foundation,* August 10, 2015, http://www.heritage.org/research/commentary/2015/8/why-iran-ideal-increases-the-risk-of-war .

154 The Heritage Foundation, "DeMint Statement on Iran Nuclear Deal," *The Heritage Foundation,* July 14, 2015, http://www.heritage.org/research/reports/2015/07/demint-statement-on-iran-nuclear-deal?ac=1 .

155 William R. Forstchen, ""EMP 101" A Basic Primer & Suggestions for Preparedness," onesecondafter.com, 2008.

156 R. James Woolsey and Peter Vincent Pry, "The Growing Threat From an EMP Attack," *The Wall Street Journal,*

http://www.wsj.com/articles/james-woolsey-and-peter-vincent-pry-the-growing-threat-from-an-emp-attack-1407885281 .

157 William R. Forstchen, ""EMP 101" A Basic Primer & Suggestions for Preparedness," onesecondafter.com, 2008.

158 Henry F. Cooper and Peter Vincent Pry, "The Threat to Melt the Electric Grid," *The Wall Street Journal,* April 30, 2015, http://www.wsj.com/articles/the-threat-to-melt-the-electric-grid-1430436815 .

159 William R. Forstchen, ""EMP 101" A Basic Primer & Suggestions for Preparedness," onesecondafter.com, 2008.

160 Joel Himelfarb, "Report: Iran Prepared for Nuclear EMP Attack on US," Newsmax Media, Inc., March 19. 2015, http://www.newsmax.com/Newsfront/iran-nuclear-emp-attack/2015/03/19/id/631333/ .

161 Henry F. Cooper and Peter Vincent Pry, "The Threat to Melt the Electric Grid," *The Wall Street Journal,* April 30, 2015, http://www.wsj.com/articles/the-threat-to-melt-the-electric-grid-1430436815 .

162 Joel Himelfarb, "Report: Iran Prepared for Nuclear EMP Attack on US," Newsmax Media, Inc., March 19. 2015, http://www.newsmax.com/Newsfront/iran-nuclear-emp-attack/2015/03/19/id/631333/ .

163 Nick Gass, "Kerry to Iran: Stop 'Death to America' chants," Politico LLC, July 24, 2015, http://www.politico.com/story/2015/07/john-kerry-iran-stop-death-to-america-120579 .

164 Adam Kredo, "Iran: 'We Welcome War With the U.S.'," The Washington Free Beacon, May 7, 2015, http://freebeacon.com/national-security/iran-we-welcome-war-with-the-u-s/ .

165 Jon Hilkevitch, "FAA outlines strategy to recover from air-traffic control outages," *Chicago Tribune,* November 24, 2014, http://www.chicagotribune.com/suburbs/aurora-beacon-news/ct-faa-chicago-center-fire-report-met-1125-20141124-story.html .

166 Ucilia Wang, "Report: The Trillion-Dollar Risk Of A Cyber Attack On U.S. Power Grid," *Forbes,* July 8, 2015, http://www.forbes.com/sites/uciliawang/2015/07/08/report-the-trillion-dollar-risk-of-a-cyber-attack-on-u-s-power-grid/ .

167 Chris Frates and Curt Devine, "Government hacks and security breaches skyrocket," Cable News Network, December 19, 2014, http://www.cnn.com/2014/12/19/politics/government-hacks-and-

security-breaches-skyrocket/ .

168 Samantha White, "Global cyber-attacks up 48% in 2014," *CGMA Magazine,* American Institute of CPAs and Chartered Institute of Management Accountants, October 8, 2014, http://www.cgma.org/magazine/news/pages/201411089.aspx .

169 Rebecca Smith, "Assault on California Power Station Raises Alarm on Potential for Terrorism," *The Wall Street Journal,* February 5, 2014, http://www.wsj.com/articles/SB10001424052702304851104579359141941621778 .

170 Rebecca Smith, "Assault on California Power Station Raises Alarm on Potential for Terrorism," *The Wall Street Journal,* February 5, 2014, http://www.wsj.com/articles/SB10001424052702304851104579359141941621778 .

171 Eric Morath, "The Worst Expansion Since World War II Was Even Weaker," *The Wall Street Journal,* http://blogs.wsj.com/economics/2015/07/30/the-worst-expansion-since-world-war-ii-was-even-weaker/?mod=WSJBlog .

172 Eric Morath, "The Worst Expansion Since World War II Was Even Weaker," *The Wall Street Journal,* http://blogs.wsj.com/economics/2015/07/30/the-worst-expansion-since-world-war-ii-was-even-weaker/?mod=WSJBlog .

173 Household Data: Table A-1. Employment status of the civilian population by sex and age, "Economic News Release," *Bureau of Labor Statistics,* September 4, 2015, http://www.bls.gov/news.release/empsit.t01.htm .

174 Series Title: (Seas) Labor Force Participation Rate, Labor Force Statistics from the Current Population Survey, "Databases, Tables & Calculators by Subject," *Bureau of Labor Statistics,* September 12, 2015, http://data.bls.gov/pdq/SurveyOutputServlet .

175 Labor Force Participation, "Topics at a Glance," *Bureau of Labor Statistics,* November 12, 2014, http://www.bls.gov/bls/cps_fact_sheets/lfp_mock.htm .

176 Household Data: Table A-15. Alternative measures of labor underutilization, "Economic News Release," *Bureau of Labor Statistics,* September 4, 2015, http://www.bls.gov/news.release/empsit.t15.htm .

177 Jane C. Timm and Tracy G. Lee, "Millions log on for Obamacare, crashing sites," October 1, 2013, MSNBC.com, http://www.msnbc.com/msnbc/millions-log-obamacare-crashing-

sites .

[178] Alex Wayne, "Obamacare Website Costs Exceed $2 Billion, Study Finds," Bloomberg.com, September 24, 2014, http://www.bloomberg.com/news/articles/2014-09-24/obamacare-website-costs-exceed-2-billion-study-finds .

[179] Louise Radnofsky and Stephanie Armour, "Insurers Win Big Health-Rate Increases," *The Wall Street Journal,* August 27, 2015, http://www.wsj.com/articles/insurers-win-big-health-rate-increases-1440628848 .

[180] Daniel Chang, "Obamacare health insurance premiums to rise 9.5 percent for 2016, state regulator reports," *Miami Herald,* August 25, 2015, http://www.miamiherald.com/news/health-care/article32430879.html .

[181] Chris Conover, "Now There Can Be No Doubt: Obamacare Has Increased Non-Group Premiums In Nearly All States," *Forbes,* October 23, 2014, http://www.forbes.com/sites/theapothecary/2014/10/23/now-there-can-be-no-doubt-obamacare-will-increase-non-group-premiums-in-nearly-all-states/ .

[182] Laura Ungar and Jayne O'Donnell, "Dilemma over deductibles: Costs crippling middle class," *USA Today,* January 1, 2015, http://www.usatoday.com/story/news/nation/2015/01/01/middle-class-workers-struggle-to-pay-for-care-despite-insurance/19841235/
.

[183] Laura Ungar and Jayne O'Donnell, "Dilemma over deductibles: Costs crippling middle class," *USA Today,* January 1, 2015, http://www.usatoday.com/story/news/nation/2015/01/01/middle-class-workers-struggle-to-pay-for-care-despite-insurance/19841235/
.

[184] Laura Ungar and Jayne O'Donnell, "Dilemma over deductibles: Costs crippling middle class," *USA Today,* January 1, 2015, http://www.usatoday.com/story/news/nation/2015/01/01/middle-class-workers-struggle-to-pay-for-care-despite-insurance/19841235/
.

[185] Trey Garrison, "MBA Servicing: Why would anyone bother to do this anymore?" HW Publishing LLC, February 24, 2015, http://www.housingwire.com/blogs/1-rewired/post/33053-mba-servicing-why-would-anyone-bother-to-do-this-anymore .

[186] Trey Garrison, "MBA Servicing: Why would anyone bother to do this anymore?" HW Publishing LLC, February 24, 2015, http://www.housingwire.com/blogs/1-rewired/post/33053-mba-

servicing-why-would-anyone-bother-to-do-this-anymore .

187 Edward Glaeser, "Land Use Restrictions and Other Barriers to Growth," *Cato Institute,* December 2014, http://www.cato.org/publications/cato-online-forum/land-use-restrictions-other-barriers-growth .

188 Edward Glaeser, "Land Use Restrictions and Other Barriers to Growth," *Cato Institute,* December 2014, http://www.cato.org/publications/cato-online-forum/land-use-restrictions-other-barriers-growth .

189 Edward Glaeser, "Land Use Restrictions and Other Barriers to Growth," *Cato Institute,* December 2014, http://www.cato.org/publications/cato-online-forum/land-use-restrictions-other-barriers-growth .

190 Clyde Wayne Crews Jr., Ten Thousand Commandments: An Annual Snapshot of the Federal Regulatory State, 2015 Edition, *Competitive Enterprise Institute,* https://cei.org/sites/default/files/10%2C000%20Commandments%20 2015%20-%2005-12-2015.pdf .

191 Gerard Francis Lameiro, *America's Economic War –Your Freedom, Money and Life: A Citizen's Handbook for Understanding the War between American Capitalism and Socialism* (Fort Collins, CO: Lameiro Economics LLC, 2009).

192 R. Hal Williams, *Realigning America: McKinley, Bryan, and the Remarkable Election of 1896* (Lawrence, KS: University Press of Kansas, 2010), pp. 137 – 138.

193 "Election 2010: House Map," *The New York Times,* http://elections.nytimes.com/2010/results/house .

194 "Election 2010: Senate Map," *The New York Times,* http://elections.nytimes.com/2010/results/senate .

195 "Election 2010: Governor Map," *The New York Times,"* http://elections.nytimes.com/2010/results/governor .

196 "HOME PAGE: STATEVOTE 2010," *National Conference of State Legislatures,* http://www.ncsl.org/research/elections-and-campaigns/statevote-2010.aspx .

197 Greg Smith, "Religion in the 2010 Elections: A Preliminary Look," *Pew Research Center,* November 3, 2010, Updated November 12, 2010, http://www.pewforum.org/2010/11/03/religion-in-the-2010-election-a-preliminary-look/ .

198 "Election 2014: Senate Election Results," *The New York Times,* http://elections.nytimes.com/2014/results/senate .

199 "Election 2014: House Election Results," *The New York Times,*

http://elections.nytimes.com/2014/results/house?utm_source=top_n
av&utm_medium=web&utm_campaign=election-2014 .
200 Donna Cassata, "GOP Matches Truman-Era High With 246
House Seats," RealClearPolitics, December 6, 2014,
http://www.realclearpolitics.com/articles/2014/12/06/gop_matches_tr
uman-era_high_with_246_house_seats_124881.html .
201 Guy Benson, "Wave, Continued: GOP Will Control 70 Percent of
All State Legislative Chambers," Townhall.com, November 6, 2014,
http://townhall.com/tipsheet/guybenson/2014/11/06/wave-gop-will-
control-more-state-legislative-chambers-than-ever-before-n1915164
.
202 Frank Newport, "Economy, Government Top Election Issues for
Both Parties," *Gallup,* October 9, 2014,
http://www.gallup.com/poll/178133/economy-government-top-
election-issues-parties.aspx .
203 Dana Blanton, "Fox News Poll: Outsiders rule 2016 GOP field,
support for Biden nearly doubles," Fox News Network, LLC,
September 24, 2015,
http://www.foxnews.com/politics/2015/09/24/fox-news-poll-outsiders-
rule-2016-gop-field-support-for-biden-nearly-doubles/ .
204 George E. Mowry, "Election of 1912," History of American
Presidential Elections 1789 – 2008, Fourth Edition, Volume II: 1872
– 1940, Gil Troy, Arthur M. Schlesinger Jr. and Fred L. Israel,
Editors (New York, NY: Facts On File, Inc., An Imprint of Infobase
Learning, 2012), pp. 877 – 907.
205 Gerard Francis Lameiro, *Renewing America and Its Heritage of
Freedom: What Freedom-Loving Americans Can Do to Help* (Fort
Collins, CO: Gerard Francis Lameiro, 2014), pp. 75 – 101.
206 Gerard Francis Lameiro, *Renewing America and Its Heritage of
Freedom: What Freedom-Loving Americans Can Do to Help* (Fort
Collins, CO: Gerard Francis Lameiro, 2014), pp. 167 – 218.
207 Gerard Francis Lameiro, *Renewing America and Its Heritage of
Freedom: What Freedom-Loving Americans Can Do to Help* (Fort
Collins, CO: Gerard Francis Lameiro, 2014), pp. 29 – 35.
208 Andrew C. McCarthy, "Congress Must Ditch the Corker Bill and
Treat the Iran Deal as Either a Treaty or Proposed Legislation to be
Voted Up or Down," The Corner, NationalReview.com, July 17,
2015, http://www.nationalreview.com/corner/421349/congress-must-
ditch-corker-bill-and-treat-iran-deal-either-treaty-or-proposed .
209 Henry F. Cooper and Peter Vincent Pry, "The Threat to Melt the
Electric Grid," *The Wall Street Journal,* April 30, 2015,

http://www.wsj.com/articles/the-threat-to-melt-the-electric-grid-1430436815 .

210 Henry F. Cooper and Peter Vincent Pry, "The Threat to Melt the Electric Grid," *The Wall Street Journal,* April 30, 2015, http://www.wsj.com/articles/the-threat-to-melt-the-electric-grid-1430436815 .

211 Henry F. Cooper and Peter Vincent Pry, "The Threat to Melt the Electric Grid," *The Wall Street Journal,* April 30, 2015, http://www.wsj.com/articles/the-threat-to-melt-the-electric-grid-1430436815 .

212 Joel Himelfarb, "Pentagon Fears North Korean Nukes Mounted on ICBMs," NewsMax Media, Inc., April 13, 2015, http://www.newsmax.com/Newsfront/North-Korea-nuclear-bomb-ICMB/2015/04/13/id/638214/ .

213 Elliot Jager, "Boeing Wants to Make a Protective 'Force Field'," NewsMax Media, Inc., March 30, 2015, http://www.newsmax.com/SciTech/force-field-boeing-patent-military/2015/03/30/id/635189/ .

214 John F. Kennedy, "Remarks of Senator John F. Kennedy, Municipal Auditorium, Canton, Ohio," September 27, 1960, John F. Kennedy, XXXV President of the United States: 1961 – 1963, Gerhard Peters and John T. Woolley - The American Presidency Project, 1999 – 2015, http://www.presidency.ucsb.edu/ws/?pid=74231 .

215 "General Electronic Benefit Transfer (EBT) Information," EBT, United States Department of Agriculture Food and Nutrition Service, http://www.fns.usda.gov/ebt/general-electronic-benefit-transfer-ebt-information .

216 John B. Taylor, "Jobs, Productivity, and Jeb Bush's Tax Plan," Economics One: A blog by John B. Taylor, September 14, 2015, http://economicsone.com/ .

217 John B. Taylor, "Jobs, Productivity, and Jeb Bush's Tax Plan," Economics One: A blog by John B. Taylor, September 14, 2015, http://economicsone.com/ .

218 Lewis Saret, "What the New 3.8% Medicare Surtax Means for You And Your Investments," *Forbes,* March 14, 2013, http://www.forbes.com/sites/lewissaret/2013/03/14/code-sec-1411-what-the-new-3-8-medicare-surtax-mean-for-you-and-your-investments/ .

219 Bill Bischoff, "How to avoid the surtax on investment income," MarketWatch, Inc., May 2, 2015,

http://www.marketwatch.com/story/how-to-avoid-the-38-medicare-surtax-on-investment-income-2015-04-28 .

220 Gerard Francis Lameiro, *Renewing America and Its Heritage of Freedom: What Freedom-Loving Americans Can Do to Help* (Fort Collins, CO: Gerard Francis Lameiro, 2014), p. 194.

221 David Malpass, "Pro-Growth Tools for the Frozen Fed," *The Wall Street Journal,* October 6, 2015, http://www.wsj.com/articles/pro-growth-tools-for-the-frozen-fed-1444169417 .

222 David Malpass, "Pro-Growth Tools for the Frozen Fed," *The Wall Street Journal,* October 6, 2015, http://www.wsj.com/articles/pro-growth-tools-for-the-frozen-fed-1444169417 .

223 Jim Clifton, "American Entrepreneurship: Dead or Alive?" Business Journal, Gallup, Inc., January 13, 2015, http://www.gallup.com/businessjournal/180431/american-entrepreneurship-dead-alive.aspx .

224 John B. Taylor, *First Principles: Five Keys to Restoring America's Prosperity* (New York, NY: W. W. Norton & Company, Inc., 2012).

225 Gerard Francis Lameiro, *America's Economic War –Your Freedom, Money and Life: A Citizen's Handbook for Understanding the War between American Capitalism and Socialism* (Fort Collins, CO: Lameiro Economics LLC, 2009), pp. 23 – 25.

226 "The One Cent Solution," Citizens for Restoring America's Financial Future, 2015, http://www.onecentsolution.org/the-one-cent-solution/ .

227 R. J. Petrella, "Medical Query: Were You Struck by a Duck?, *The Wall Street Journal,* October 13, 2015, http://www.wsj.com/articles/medical-query-were-you-struck-by-a-duck-1444776711 .

228 R. J. Petrella, "Medical Query: Were You Struck by a Duck?, *The Wall Street Journal,* October 13, 2015, http://www.wsj.com/articles/medical-query-were-you-struck-by-a-duck-1444776711 .

229 R. J. Petrella, "Medical Query: Were You Struck by a Duck?, *The Wall Street Journal,* October 13, 2015, http://www.wsj.com/articles/medical-query-were-you-struck-by-a-duck-1444776711 .

230 Ravi Somaiya, "Layoffs Begin at The Times After Buyouts Come Up Short," *The New York Times,* December 16, 2014,

http://www.nytimes.com/2014/12/17/business/layoffs-new-york-times.html .

231 Jordan Chariton, "Layoffs Loom Over LA Times, Tribune Publishing Announces Buyouts Program," The Wrap News Inc., October 5, 2015, http://www.thewrap.com/tribune-publishing-launches-buyouts-program/ .

232 "A round of layoffs at the Boston Globe," *Media Life Magazine,* October 15, 2015, http://www.medialifemagazine.com/a-round-of-layoffs-at-boston-globe/ .

233 Jonathan Capehart, "'Hands up, don't shoot' was built on a lie," *The Washington Post,* March 16, 2015, http://www.washingtonpost.com/blogs/post-partisan/wp/2015/03/16/lesson-learned-from-the-shooting-of-michael-brown/ .

234 Ronald Reagan, "The Crusade for Freedom," Address to the British Parliament, House of Commons, London, June 8, 1982, *The Greatest Speeches of Ronald Reagan: Introduction by Michael Reagan, 2nd Edition* (West Palm Beach, FL: NewsMax.com, Inc., 2001, "With introduction by Michael Reagan," NewsMax.com, 2002), pp. 107 – 114.

235 Rush Limbaugh, "The Conservative-Media Revolution Has Forced the Liberal Media to Abandon Any Pretense of Objectivity," *National Review,* November 4, 2015, http://www.nationalreview.com/article/426529/rush-limbaugh-national-review-conservative-media-revolution .

236 Rush Limbaugh, "The Conservative-Media Revolution Has Forced the Liberal Media to Abandon Any Pretense of Objectivity," *National Review,* November 4, 2015, http://www.nationalreview.com/article/426529/rush-limbaugh-national-review-conservative-media-revolution .

237 Homeland Security and Governmental Affairs Committee, United States Senate, "Senate Report 114-94 - PRESIDENTIAL TRANSITIONS IMPROVEMENTS ACT OF 2015," Congress.Gov, July 27, 2015, https://www.congress.gov/congressional-report/114th-congress/senate-report/94/1 .

238 Homeland Security and Governmental Affairs Committee, United States Senate, "Senate Report 114-94 - PRESIDENTIAL TRANSITIONS IMPROVEMENTS ACT OF 2015," Congress.Gov, July 27, 2015, https://www.congress.gov/congressional-report/114th-congress/senate-report/94/1 .

239 Robert Longley, "Presidential Appointments: No Senate

Required," About.com, 2015,
http://usgovinfo.about.com/od/thepresidentandcabinet/a/Presidentia
l-Appointments-No-Senate-Required.htm .

240 Robert Longley, "Presidential Appointments: No Senate
Required," About.com, 2015,
http://usgovinfo.about.com/od/thepresidentandcabinet/a/Presidentia
l-Appointments-No-Senate-Required.htm .

241 Carl M. Brauer, *Presidential Transitions: Eisenhower through
Reagan* (New York, NY: Oxford University Press, Inc., President
and Fellows of Harvard College, 1986), pp. 217 – 255.

242 Carl M. Brauer, *Presidential Transitions: Eisenhower through
Reagan* (New York, NY: Oxford University Press, Inc., President
and Fellows of Harvard College, 1986), pp. 217 – 255.

243 Carl M. Brauer, *Presidential Transitions: Eisenhower through
Reagan* (New York, NY: Oxford University Press, Inc., President
and Fellows of Harvard College, 1986), pp. 256 – 268.

244 William McKinley's First Inaugural Address, March 4, 1897.
Please see: R. Hal Williams, *Realigning America: McKinley, Bryan,
and the Remarkable Election of 1896* (Lawrence, KS: University
Press of Kansas, 2010), pp. 188 – 196.

245 Carl M. Brauer, *Presidential Transitions: Eisenhower through
Reagan* (New York, NY: Oxford University Press, Inc., President
and Fellows of Harvard College, 1986), pp. 256 – 268.

246 Carl M. Brauer, *Presidential Transitions: Eisenhower through
Reagan* (New York, NY: Oxford University Press, Inc., President
and Fellows of Harvard College, 1986), pp. 256 – 268.

247 Ronald Reagan, "The Crusade for Freedom," Address to the
British Parliament, House of Commons, London, June 8, 1982, *The
Greatest Speeches of Ronald Reagan: Introduction by Michael
Reagan, 2nd Edition* (West Palm Beach, FL: NewsMax.com, Inc.,
2001, "With introduction by Michael Reagan," NewsMax.com,
2002), pp. 107 – 114.

248 Ronald Reagan, "The Crusade for Freedom," Address to the
British Parliament, House of Commons, London, June 8, 1982, *The
Greatest Speeches of Ronald Reagan: Introduction by Michael
Reagan, 2nd Edition* (West Palm Beach, FL: NewsMax.com, Inc.,
2001, "With introduction by Michael Reagan," NewsMax.com,
2002), pp. 107 – 114.

249 John F. Kennedy, "Remarks of Senator John F. Kennedy,
Municipal Auditorium, Canton, Ohio," September 27, 1960, John F.
Kennedy, XXXV President of the United States: 1961 – 1963,

Gerhard Peters and John T. Woolley - The American Presidency Project, 1999 – 2015, http://www.presidency.ucsb.edu/ws/?pid=74231 .